Introduction

B1 Preliminary *for Schools*

B1 Preliminary *for Schools* is an intermediate level qualification in practical everyday English language skills. It follows on as a progression from A2 Key and it can help give learners confidence to go on and study for taking higher level Cambridge English Qualifications such as B2 First.
It is aimed at school students who want to show they can:

- read simple textbooks and articles in English
- respond to emails on everyday subjects
- understand factual information
- show awareness of opinions and mood in spoken and written English.

The B1 Preliminary *for Schools* certificate is recognised around the world as proof of intermediate level English skills for industrial, administrative and service-based employment. It is also accepted by a wide range of educational institutions for study purposes.

Exam format in detail
The updated exam is made up of four papers developed to test your English skills. You can see exactly what's in each paper below.

Paper	Content	Marks (% of total)	Purpose
Reading (45 minutes)	6 parts / 32 questions	25%	Shows you can read and understand the main points from signs, newspapers and magazines.
Writing (45 minutes)	2 parts / 3 questions	25%	Shows you can write a variety of text types, with a focus on organisation, structure and accuracy of language to clearly communicate your message.
Listening (30 minutes, including 6 minutes' transfer time)	4 parts / 25 questions	25%	Shows you can follow and understand a range of spoken materials including announcements and discussions about everyday life.
Speaking (12 minutes per pair of candidates)	4 parts	25%	Shows how good your spoken English is as you take part in conversation by asking/answering questions and talking, for example, about your likes and dislikes. Your Speaking test will be conducted face to face with one or two other candidates and two examiners. This makes your test more realistic and more reliable.

Introduction

Paper 1	Reading	45 minutes
Part & task	**Format**	**No. of Questions**
Part 1 Multiple-choice short texts	Understanding five short messages of different types.	5
Part 2 Matching	Match five descriptions of people to eight short texts, reading for specific information and detailed comprehension.	5
Part 3 Multiple choice	Read to understand gist, global and detailed meaning, attitude, opinions and feelings, and answer five multiple-choice questions with four options (A, B, C, D).	5
Part 4 Gapped text	Read to understand gist and text structure: choose the correct sentence to put in the gaps.	5
Part 5 Multiple-choice cloze	Read a text and choose missing words (A, B, C, D) to fill in the gaps.	6
Part 6 Open gap cloze	Read a text and write one word in each gap.	6

Paper 2	Writing	45 minutes
Part & task	**Format**	**No. of Questions**
Part 1 Write an email	Write an email in response to information given (about 100 words).	1
Part 2 Write an article or story	Write either an article or a story on the topic given (about 100 words).	1

Introduction

Paper 3	Listening	Approx 30 minutes
Part & task	Format	No. of Questions
Part 1 Multiple-choice short texts	Listen to seven short texts for specific information and choose the right picture (A, B, C).	7
Part 2 Multiple-choice short texts	Listen to six short dialogues for attitudes and opinions, and choose the right option (A, B, C).	6
Part 3 Gap fill	Listen to a longer text and write down missing information in the gaps.	6
Part 4 Multiple-choice long text	Listen to a longer text for specific information, detailed meaning, attitudes and opinions.	6

Paper 4	Speaking	12 minutes
Part & task	Format	Minutes per part
Part 1 Introductory phase	Candidates show ability to use general interactional and social language.	2-3 minutes
Part 2 Individual long turn	Describing photographs and managing discourse, using appropriate vocabulary in a longer turn.	2-3 minutes
Part 3 Collaborative task	Using functional language to make and respond to suggestions, discuss alternatives, make recommendations and negotiate agreement, based on picture prompts.	2-3 minutes
Part 4 Discussion	Talking about likes/dislikes, preferences, habits, opinions and agreeing/disagreeing. Part 4 is now linked to the collaborative task.	3 minutes

Test 1 Paper 1 Reading

Part 1

Questions 1-5

For each question, choose the correct answer.

1

FOR SAFETY REASONS
ALL VISITORS,
BOTH CHILDREN AND ADULTS,
MUST RECEIVE A PASS
AT THE OFFICE IN ORDER
TO ENTER THE SCHOOL

A You may not access the school unless you have a pass.

B Children are only allowed to enter the school with an adult visitor.

C You must only enter the school if you are a child's parent.

2

This medicine should be taken with plenty of water on an empty stomach.

A Do not eat anything before taking the medicine.

B You must drink a lot of water after you have taken the medicine.

C This medicine can cause a stomach ache if you drink it.

3

55p fare
no change given
on the bus

A You can't use cash to buy the ticket on the bus.

B Tickets aren't sold on the bus.

C You must have the exact amount of money for the ticket.

Paper 1 Reading — Test 1

4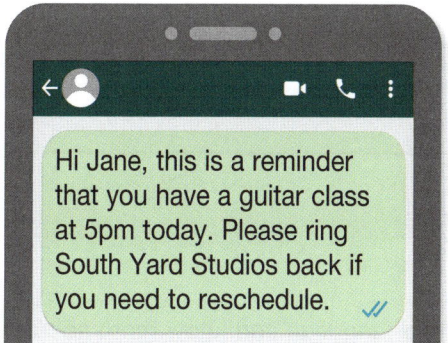

Hi Jane, this is a reminder that you have a guitar class at 5pm today. Please ring South Yard Studios back if you need to reschedule.

A Text a message if you are late for class.

B You must call before your lesson at South Yard Studios.

C Don't forget that you have an appointment in the afternoon.

5

FOR SALE
Toyama Game Console 3X
bought last week
played twice
ship in one day

The ad says that the console

A can only be used by two players.

B is brand new.

C can be sent to the buyer.

Exam tips
Don't just look for individual words with similar meaning in the text and the options. When you choose your answer, make sure the whole meaning makes sense.

Guidance for candidates
In Reading Part 1 candidates must read five short texts and match them with the correct option A, B or C.

They should think of what **kind of text** they are reading. For example, texts 1 and 3 are both notices. What kind of text is text 2?

☐ a road sign   ☐ a label   ☐ an advertisement   ☐ an email or text message

They should also think of the **purpose** of each text. For example, what is the purpose of text 4?

☐ to warn Jane about something   ☐ to advise Jane to do something   ☐ to remind Jane to do something

Some texts may contain words candidates don't know yet. In this case:
- they should check which two options are wrong, or
- they can try to guess the meaning from the kind of text and situation they find it in.

For example, what does the word 'ship' mean in text 5? _____

5

Test 1 Paper 1 Reading

Part 2

Questions 6-10

For each question, choose the correct answer.

The people below all want to learn a new language.
On the opposite page there are descriptions of eight language courses.
Decide which course would be the most suitable for the people below.

6

Tanya would like to learn an oriental language and know more about Asian culture. She can attend classes twice a week for up to six months. She enjoys learning in little groups and wants to get an end-course certificate.

7

Haruki's going to start an international high school in England. He studied Japanese at a junior high school but he needs to brush it up before the entrance test. He wants to improve his speaking and he'd prefer one-to-one lessons around lunch time.

8

Kate and her mother Lara are planning to learn a European foreign language in the same class. Lara is at school in the morning so she can only do an afternoon course. She would like to find email pen pals that she can visit in their country.

9

Rajani is fond of archaeology. He would like to learn Latin or Greek to help him improve his knowledge of past civilisations. He doesn't have much time so he is looking for an afternoon beginner course that will help him to read aloud real works from the classics.

10

Gabriel is a 16-year-old boy whose parents are planning a trip to the Far East next summer. He would like to learn an Asian language and he's looking for classes with people the same age as him. He also wants to learn how to write and read characters.

Language Courses

A Getting started on classical Greek

This 10-hour course is for first-time learners of Greek who would like to start studying a classical language. After learning about the main grammar and pronunciation rules of this language, students are offered the chance to put in some early practice. Every Monday from 5 to 7 p.m.

B Hebrew reading course

This intensive course will examine the history of this unique language from its early origins to its modern form as well as its influence on the Greek and Latin alphabets. You will also learn how to recognise the letters in ancient inscriptions and understand word structure. Lessons are three times a week from 8 to 10 a.m.

C Latin courses in Cambridge

Join our weekly morning classes, which run for 20 weeks over two terms: the classes are limited to a maximum of 12 students, to make sure every student gets the necessary attention to learn Latin. We offer courses at levels 1-3, suitable for both beginners and advanced Latin speakers.

D Mandarin classes at the 'Ni Hao Language Centre'

This school offers both one-on-one lessons or small classes for up to 3 times a week. In about half a year students can learn to speak Mandarin and get ready for the HSK national exam. We also provide a list of host families in China if you plan to travel there at the end of the course.

E Learning Japanese in England

This elementary-level Japanese course, consisting of 30 evening lessons over 15 weeks, is designed for people who want to learn basic everyday life expressions. Each lesson covers dialogues, vocabulary, grammar, quizzes and role plays. After completing this course, you will be able to talk about simple topics and know about Japanese culture.

F Intensive Japanese

Need to refresh your vocabulary and conversation skills in Japanese? Join our crash course for intermediate learners and improve your pronunciation with a personal mother-tongue tutor: in a fortnight you will be able to talk about a selection of topics from hobbies to schoolwork. Classes can be arranged to fit your schedules.

G Korean School of London

Our Korean language program includes both teenage and children courses every Thursday and Saturday morning from January to June. The classes will focus on speaking, listening and vocabulary exercises to provide everyday speaking skills, but teenage students will also learn to read and write a few characters.

H A taste of Sweden

This course is open to teenagers and adults who want to learn Swedish and join our 2-week exchange programme in Stockholm. Students will learn how to communicate with people in common everyday situations. Classes are from 3.30 to 5.00 p.m. every Thursday, but you can practise online with your host family in Sweden, too.

Paper 1 Reading

Part 3

Questions 11-15

For each question, choose the correct answer.

Let's sing along!
13-year-old Helena Hutchinsons talks about the benefits of singing

Have you ever wondered why people often catch themselves singing while having a shower or making dinner? Or why karaoke has been popular since it appeared in the 1980s? We still have to understand a lot about the effects of music on our brain, but many studies already show it is good for our mind and our body alike.

The first reason you feel like singing along when you listen to a song is that it makes you feel less lonely. Whether you are cycling home, doing your homework or cheering at your favourite pop star's concert, singing is communication. It is like sharing a moment with the singer or the people around you: this is why babies often stop crying when they hear music and all children enjoy singing.

All types of singing can make you feel better, but group singing has the best effects on people's lives. Singing in a group in front of a crowd builds confidence, which explains why joining a choir can decrease anxiety in depressed patients. When you sing, it's nearly impossible to think about other things. Since you must focus on what you are doing, singing stops you being worried about stressful situations.

Singing can also improve speech development. Children learn to speak faster if they regularly sing from an early age and they are often better at communicating through language. When you sing you need to remember words and tunes, so this activity is also an excellent way to learn a foreign language and make your pronunciation sound more natural.

You can also improve your physical health when you sing. Since you need to breathe properly, when you sing you breathe out more carbon dioxide and take in more oxygen, which makes your body fitter and stronger against illnesses. So if you decide to take up a new hobby, singing could be the best way for you to have fun, make new friends and improve your health at the same time.

Exam tips
Most questions follow the order of the information given in the paragraphs of the texts.

Guidance for candidates
In Reading Part 3 candidates must read a text and then choose an option (A, B, C or D) to answer five questions. They should:

- read the title and the text quickly to find out what it is about
- read each paragraph carefully and underline any part that seems to match the questions
- remember that some questions may refer to the general meaning (the writer's topic or the purpose of the text).

Paper 1 Reading — Test 1

11 The first paragraph says that

- **A** people prefer singing when they have a meal.
- **B** singing can help us understand the brain better.
- **C** we can improve our health when we sing.
- **D** karaoke isn't as popular as in the 1980s.

12 What happens when you sing along to a song?

- **A** It makes you feel connected to others.
- **B** It's like being at the concert of your favourite singer.
- **C** You may feel like a pop star.
- **D** Children develop their musicality when they listen to a song.

13 What does the writer say about joining a choir?

- **A** It helps you when you perform in a crowded building.
- **B** It makes you feel less depressed in front of an audience.
- **C** You can't sing unless you are relaxed.
- **D** You will be able to solve your everyday problems.

14 Singing can help children

- **A** not to take in carbon dioxide.
- **B** to increase their communication skills.
- **C** to spell words properly.
- **D** to learn the words of a song.

15 Which of the following sums up the ideas in the article?

A
You should sing with other people if you want to have fun and improve your health.

B
People who are fond of singing have more friends than those who don't enjoy singing.

C
There are several positive effects on how you feel when you take up singing as a hobby.

D
Children that don't like singing may not be as confident as those that join a choir.

Part 4

Questions 16-20

Five sentences have been removed from the text below.
For each space, choose the correct answer.
There are three extra sentences which you do not need to use.

Interactive films
by Terry P. Roham, aged 15

Interactive cinema is a form of entertainment which mixes traditional filmmaking and video game technology. In an interactive movie, the audience is given the power to decide what choices the main character must make at crucial moments of the story. **16**

Though most people think it is a very recent invention, the first interactive film, *Kinoautomat*, was made by a Czech director in the 1960s. In this early version, the movie was interrupted and the audience was asked to choose between the two possible scenes and to vote for the one they wanted to be shown next. **17**

It was after the invention of CD-ROMs that game developers started to realise they could combine traditional filming methods and new technological possibilities. This is how movie makers started to film live actors on a green screen. **18**

In the 2000s there were new attempts at creating interactive movies. **19** One of the main problems was the limited options the viewers had in giving shape to their own plot and conclusion. However, things seem to have changed since the recent release of *Bandersnatch*. **20**
With its 6 viewer options and 5 different endings the episode has received favourable reviews from both critic and the audience.

Paper 1 Reading — Test 1

A A short tutorial explains to the viewer how to make choices.

B Despite this, people appeared to lose interest in the genre.

C But then something unusual happens.

D Whatever decision was made, however, the film ending was the same.

E It is an interactive episode of a popular sci-fi series that came out in 2018.

F The filmed scene could then be moved onto a chosen digital background.

G But the idea itself is even older.

H Since there are different possible developments, the end depends on each viewer.

Exam tips
In Reading Part 4, read the whole text carefully to understand the meaning.
When you choose your answer, pay attention to:

- words like *this*, *these*, *it*, *they*, etc. in the missing sentences: they refer to something mentioned before so it will be easier to link them to the rest
- verb tenses in the missing sentences: do they follow a logical order?

Guidance for candidates
Look at the sentences before and after the gap: they often contain words or phrases that refer to the missing sentence.
After selecting a sentence, candidates should check why the other sentences do not fit.
Once they have chosen all the missing sentences, candidates should read the text once more to make sure the whole text makes sense.

Test 1 Paper 1 Reading

Part 5

Questions 21-26

For each question, choose the correct answer.

Online shopping
vs
Traditional shopping

In today's world there is hardly anyone who (21) _____ never bought anything online. Shopping online allows us to find whatever we want to buy and is now more popular than ever. You just need to create an account and look (22) _____ the items which loads of online stores offer. All you have to do when you are ready is click the 'enter' key and wait for the courier to bring you (23) _____ you paid for.

However, the number of people who refuse to become slaves of technology and consumerism is increasing: they keep (24) _____ most of their shopping traditionally. They think that (25) _____ they lose a lot of time going to the right shop, they can check the item, try on clothes and know where the product comes from. They know online shopping has (26) _____ advantages but they still prefer traditional shopping as a way to help local businesses to keep their jobs despite the competition they have to face now.

21	**A** is	**B** had	**C** does	**D** has
22	**A** up	**B** like	**C** for	**D** after
23	**A** which	**B** whose	**C** what	**D** that
24	**A** receiving	**B** doing	**C** making	**D** taking
25	**A** despite	**B** if	**C** unless	**D** although
26	**A** much	**B** many	**C** a lot	**D** too

Exam tips
Read the text quickly to understand the general meaning.
When the missing word is a preposition, look at the words before and / or after it to help you (e.g. listen to, interested in, better than, etc.).
Always read the whole sentence before choosing an answer. Don't stop at the gap!

Guidance for candidates
In this part of the test, candidates must choose between four options which could be:
- words with a similar meaning (e.g. work / job, as / like)
- verbs which are part of fixed phrases (e.g. make your bed, take a photo)
- grammar words (relative pronouns, auxiliaries, linking words, etc.).

Candidates should look carefully at the words before and after the gap to check what kind of word is missing (a verb, a preposition, a pronoun, etc.).

Paper 1 Reading **Test 1**

Part 6

Questions 27-32

For each question, write the correct answer.
Write **one** word for each gap.

Farm Working Holidays

If you don't mind working (**27**) _____ your hands and would like to have an eco-friendly holiday while learning English, working on a farm is a great way to travel for free and enjoy the beauty of the countryside. Our farm volunteer scheme involves a lot of farms (**28**) _____ part in eco-friendly projects which are looking for teenagers to volunteer in exchange for free morning language courses, accommodation and food.

Most farm owners ask their guests to stay for at (**29**) _____ two weeks, but many guests decide to spend the whole season there in (**30**) _____ to learn everything about organic farming. Volunteers can do anything, from picking grapes to (**31**) _____ after crops. They will also milk cows or feed chickens. Working days are usually five hours (**32**) _____ day, but you may also work less.

To learn more about World Wide Opportunities on Organic Farms, check our website www.wwoof.org listing all the farms in our project.

Exam tips
Remember that words like *doesn't* are actually two words (*does + not*), so you can't use them to fill a gap. Sometimes there is more than one possible words for a gap: choose the one you prefer to fill the gap.

Guidance for candidates
In Reading Part 6 the words to find are often grammar words. Here's a simple exercise to make sure students can recognise each of them.

Match the example words on the left with each category on the right:

1 whose   A ☐ quantifier
2 an   B ☐ preposition
3 few   C ☐ auxiliary
4 would   D ☐ modal verb
5 with   E ☐ pronoun
6 were   F ☐ article

Other possible words are parts of collocations, phrasal verbs, linking words, adverbial phrases: to test candidates' knowledge, here's another exercise.

Complete the following sentences with one word. The category of word is given in brackets.

1 My father _____ up smoking because it was bad for his health. (phrasal verb)
2 I _____ my bed every morning. (collocation)
3 He studied really hard _____ he passed the test. (linking word)
4 I didn't win anything but _____ least I had fun. (adverbial phrase)

Test 1 Paper 2 Writing

Part 1

You **must** answer this question.
Write your answers in about **100 words** on the answer sheet.

Question 1

Read this email from your friend Amy and the notes you have made.

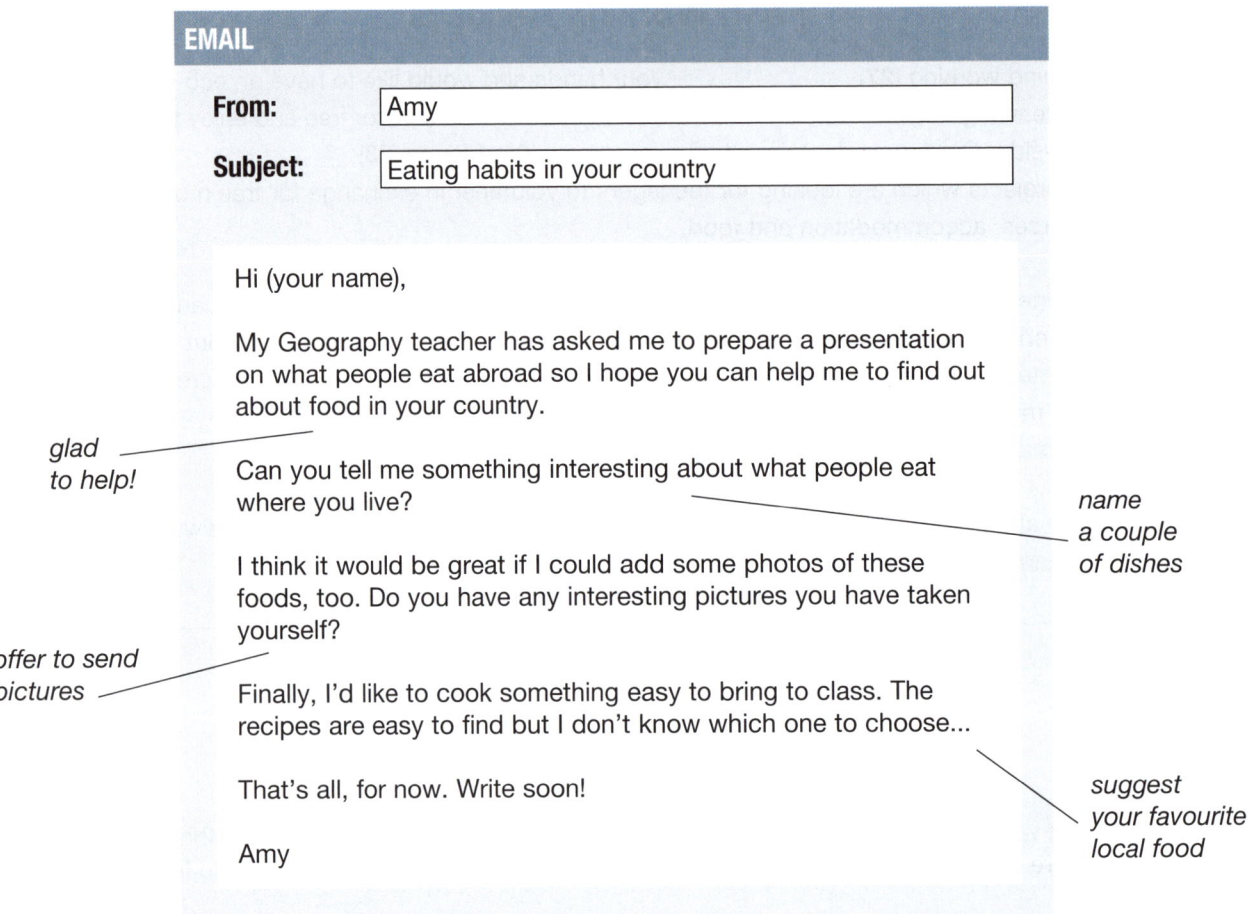

Write your **email** to your friend Amy using **all the notes**.

Exam tips
Make sure you respond to all the questions and / or prompts in the question.
Check that you have enough words.
Read through your answer at the end and check your spelling and punctuation.
Don't forget to start your email with a suitable greeting (e.g. *Dear Pam, Hi Sue*).
You must also close the message with an ending (*Best wishes, See you soon*, etc.)

Guidance for candidates
Candidates should practice how to divide their email into paragraphs and use all the notes pointing to the parts of the test.
Also, they should remember how to express different functions. To help them practice, here's a simple exercise.
Match the following phrases with their correct function:

giving your opinion	advising	suggesting what to do together	offering to do something
1 Why don't you _____	2 I'll _____	3 Shall we _____	4 I think the best _____

Paper 2 Writing — Test 1

Part 2

Choose **one** of these questions.
Write your answers in about **100 words** on the answer sheet.

Question 2

You see this advertisement in a fitness magazine.

HEALTH AND SPORT

What do you do to keep fit?
Is physical exercise enough to be healthy?
Why / Why not?
Write an article answering these questions and we will put the best one in next month's issue.

Write your **article**.

Question 3

Your English teacher has asked you to write a story.
Your story must begin with this sentence.

> When I opened the door, all I could see was a parcel on the doormat.

Write your **story**.

Exam tips
Pay attention to the questions in the article. They usually ask you to write about your personal experience. In this case, you should write about the sports you do to keep fit. Try and include a range of language related to sport, e.g. work out, play tennis, go swimming, etc.

Guidance for candidates
To write a successful **article**, candidates should follow these points:

- read the question instructions carefully
- write three short paragraphs to answer each of the three questions
- give their personal opinion using phrases like *In my opinion, I think..., I believe...*
- include examples from their experience.

Test 1 — Paper 3 Listening

Part 1

 Questions 1-7

For each question, choose the correct answer.

1 What did Jack do yesterday afternoon?

A ☐

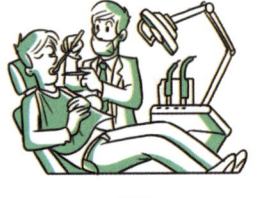

B ☐

C ☐

2 Why was the train cancelled?

A ☐

B ☐

C ☐

3 What time does the German lesson usually start on Thursdays?

A ☐

B ☐

C ☐

Exam tips
Read the question carefully and think about the kind of words you might hear.
Don't just listen for individual words, listen for the whole meaning.

Guidance for candidates
In this part of the test candidates must focus on the topic of each recording. The speakers often:

- talk about the weather
- arrange to meet somewhere or to do something at specific times
- talk about where an object is at home
- talk about places around town
- describe people or buildings
- must choose foods or drink
- talk about clothes

16

Paper 3 Listening — Test 1

4 Where are Sarah and her family having their holiday this summer?

A ☐   B ☐   C ☐

5 Where are Mum's keys?

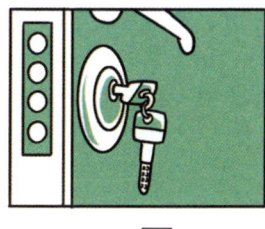  

A ☐   B ☐   C ☐

6 Who is Aidan's History teacher?

A ☐   B ☐   C ☐

7 Which photo does Cindy prefer?

A ☐   B ☐   C ☐

Test 1 Paper 3 Listening

Part 2

 Questions 8-13

For each question, choose the correct answer.

8   You will hear a boy talking about housework: what does he dislike doing?
    A   washing the dishes
    B   cleaning the windows
    C   tidying his sister's bedroom

9   You will hear two students talking about a concert. What do they agree about?
    A   the guitarist wasn't as good as expected
    B   the singer was too loud
    C   the volume was too high

10 You will hear two friends talking about a new sports centre. When did they sign up?
    A   one week ago
    B   two weeks ago
    C   three weeks ago

11 You will hear a man arranging to meet his daughter after school. What time are they going to meet?
    A   3:45
    B   4:30
    C   5:00

12 You will hear a conversation between two students on a school trip. What are they talking about?
    A   a church
    B   a tower
    C   a bridge

13 You will hear a teacher talking to her students. What does she want them to do?
    A   write an essay
    B   make an online presentation
    C   send in a review

Exam tips
Always listen to the whole conversation before making your choice. If you are not sure about an answer, remember you will always hear the recording twice.

Guidance for candidates
In this part of the test you will hear six dialogues where people often:

- give their opinion about something or someone
- talk about what they plan or would like to do
- agree or disagree about something.

Candidates should focus more on the opinions, thoughts and feelings expressed rather than what actually happens.

Paper 3 Listening — Test 1

Part 3

 Questions 14–19

For each question, write the correct answer in the gap.
Write **one** or **two words** or a **number** or a **date** or a **time**.

You will hear a woman talking about a cruise ship.

The Sea Lady

Main Facts

Built in: **(14)** _____
First tour: The Mediterranean Sea
Length of the ship: **(15)** _____ long
Can carry: 2,500 passengers and 1,700 staff

On-board Facilities

Rainbow deck
 - daytime: a large area with two pools and three hot tubs where passengers can **(16)** _____ or relax
 - nighttime: music and light show

Dinner
three dining rooms – cuisine from Japan, Italy and France
time: **(17)** _____ p.m. to 9.30 p.m.

Cloud Nine Deck
movie theatre (film begins at 10:00 p.m.)
(offering popcorn, ice cream and fresh **(18)** _____)

Visit our website at **(19)** _____ .com

Exam tips
Listen to the spelling of unknown words and practice writing them down correctly.
Write any numbers you hear as numerals, not words. It's easier!

Guidance for candidates
In this part of the test there is a person talking about a place to visit (a museum, a gallery, a holiday resort, etc.) or a plan (a school trip, a camping holiday, etc.).

Candidates will usually have to fill at least two gaps with:
 • numbers (dates, times of the day, years, sizes, etc.)
 • websites or email addresses, which are spelt out by the speaker.

Sometimes both the singular and the plural form of a word are accepted, unless there is a quantifier (a, an, some, etc.).
Smaller numbers and dates can be written in different forms (nine or 9, 12th or twelfth, March 2 or the second of March, or 2/3, etc.).

Test 1 Paper 3 Listening

Part 4

 Questions 20-25

For each question, choose the correct answer.

You will hear an interview with a manga artist talking about his job.

20 How did Masayoshi become interested in manga?
   A He started drawing his two sisters' dolls.
   B His grandfather taught him to draw.
   C He learnt to draw on his own.

21 'Cherry Blossoms in the Snow' was
   A sometimes difficult to write.
   B the work that made him win the 1992 prize.
   C a 35 volume series.

22 What do his first two series have in common?
   A They both contain many supernatural characters.
   B They tell about a similar historical period.
   C They are about sisters fighting with each other.

23 What inspires the artist for his characters?
   A people from his own family
   B both real people and ancient legends
   C famous heroes from the past

24 What has helped manga to become so popular?
   A Cosplay has increased the interest in Japanese cartoons.
   B Children can learn Japanese culture through manga.
   C In some western countries adults often enjoy reading comics.

25 What does Masayoshi suggest doing when drawing manga?
   A try to surprise the audience
   B use a science fiction setting
   C avoid too much imagination

Exam tips
The questions you have to answer follow the same order as the interviewer's questions. If you are not sure about an answer use a pencil to circle the possible answers and focus when you listen again.

Guidance for candidates
In this part of the test candidates listen to someone interviewing a person. Candidates should read the questions first to get an understanding of what the interview will be about. They will need to have a detailed understanding of the interview text to answer the questions correctly.

Paper 4 Speaking — Test 1

Part 1 (2-3 minutes)

Phase 1

The interlocutor asks the same questions to candidate A and candidate B.

Interlocutor   Good afternoon.
Can I have your mark sheets, please?
I'm (*interlocutor's name*) and this is (*assessor's name*).

What's your name?
How old are you?

	Back-up Prompts
Where do you come from?	Do you live in *name of town/city/region*?
Are you a student?	Do you study?
What do you study?	What subject do you study?

Thank you.

Phase 2

The interlocutor asks some personal questions to each candidate.
Ask Candidate A first.

Back-up Prompts

Interlocutor   **Candidate A**

What did you do yesterday evening?	Did you do anything yesterday evening? What?
Would you like to live in a different country?	Do you want to live in a different country? Why?
Why? / Why not?	

Candidate B

What's your favourite subject at school?	What subject do you like best?
Do you think that English will be useful for you in the future? Why?	Will you use English in the future? Why / Why not?

Thank you.

Exam tips
In first phase of Speaking Part 1, the questions are about your personal details, your daily life and likes and dislikes. Try and use this time to relax!
You are expected to give short but articulate answers (no one-word answers), so it's not necessary to speak too much in this phase.

Guidance for candidates
Candidates should practice the best way to answer questions such as 'What do you study?'. What could the ideal answer be among these ones?

A ☐ Maths
B ☐ I study several subjects and English, of course.
C ☐ I study English, Maths, Geography, History, PE, Science. My favourite subject is Maths, but I also like English very much because I think it's very useful and I really like it.

Test 1 Paper 4 Speaking

Part 2 (2-3 minutes)

The interlocutor gives each candidate a photograph with a different topic.

Interlocutor Now I'd like each of you to talk on your own about something. I'm going to give each of you a photograph and I'd like you to talk about it.
A, here is your photograph. It shows **friends doing something together**.
B, you just listen.
A, please tell us what you can see in the photograph.

A

Back-up prompts
- Talk about the people/person.
- Talk about the place.
- Talk about other things in the photograph.

Interlocutor Thank you.

Interlocutor B, here is your photograph. It shows **some people reading**.
A, you just listen.
B, please tell us what you can see in the photograph.

B

Back-up prompts
- Talk about the people/person.
- Talk about the place.
- Talk about other things in the photograph.

Interlocutor Thank you.

Exam tips
Speaking Part 2 is to show what vocabulary you know so focus on what words you know and what you can describe. Don't worry about trying to describe everything you see.
If you can't remember a word, try and think of other ways to say the same thing.

Paper 4 Speaking — Test 1

Part 3 (2-3 minutes)

Interlocutor Now, in this part of the test you're going to talk about something together for about two minutes. I'm going to describe a situation to you.

**Your French teacher is going to retire. You would like to give her a present.
Here are some things you could give her as presents.
Talk together and say which present would be the best for her.**

All right? Now, talk together.

Part 4 (3 minutes)

The interlocutor asks questions related to what candidates discussed in Part 3.

Interlocutor What kind of presents do you like giving to older people?
What's the most unusual present you have received?
When do people exchange presents in your country?
Where do you prefer shopping for presents?
Do you prefer to get hand-made presents or experiences (theatre, trips, concerts, etc.)?

Thank you. That is the end of the test.

Select any of the following prompts, as appropriate:
- **How/What about you?**
- **Do you agree?**
- **What do you think?**

Test 2 Paper 1 Reading

Part 1

Questions 1-5

For each question, choose the correct answer.

1

> Sam, I've run out of eggs and need you to buy a dozen. Could you get them by 6 this evening? Thanks, Mum.

A Sam has to buy eggs for a dozen guests as soon as he can.

B There are no eggs left so Sam has to get some.

C Sam's mother wants him to buy 6 eggs.

2

> **The Kebab Kingdom**
> £3 minimum charge per person between midday and 2 unless you have a reservation

A Eating at the Kebab Kingdom only costs £3 at lunchtime.

B You can have lunch for less than £3 if you have a reservation.

C People who have booked in advance don't have any extra charge to pay.

Exam tips
Always read the three options (A, B or C) carefully and compare each of them to the text. Once you've chosen the best option, read the text again to check it.

Guidance for candidates
Make sure candidates understand the meaning of the texts, even if they don't know all the words they contain.

As an example, they can answer questions such as:

- What does the expression 'run out' mean in text 1?
- Do you know an expression that means the same as 'make a reservation'?
- What's the meaning of the phrasal verb 'pick up' in text 3?
- Which information in text 4 do you have to focus on?
- Why is the receipt important in text 5?

Paper 1 Reading — Test 2

3

EMAIL

To: Brenda
From: Pete

Hi Brenda,
I've booked the theatre tickets for tomorrow's show online. Please, pick them up on your way home.
Pete

What does Pete want Brenda to do?

A Reserve two tickets for tomorrow's show.

B Collect the theatre tickets.

C Pick him up to go to the theatre together.

4

Due to building work the canteen will be closed until further notice

A Only building workers can eat at the canteen now.

B The canteen is closed when staff are working.

C You will be informed when the canteen is open.

5

THE EPIC GAME STORE
SAVE YOUR RECEIPT!
NO REFUNDS OR EXCHANGES WITHOUT ONE

A You can't return any item unless you have a receipt.

B Keep your receipt if you want to get a discount.

C The shop won't give you a receipt if you exchange items.

Test 2 Paper 1 Reading

Part 2

Questions 6-10

For each question, choose the correct answer.

The people below are all looking for information about the past.
On the opposite page there are descriptions of eight websites.
Decide which one would be the most suitable for each of them.

6  Soo-Yun needs to find some key facts about 19th-century literature. She would also like to test her knowledge of the greatest writers of the time and their works.

7  François wants to learn about Victorian society. He is looking for a website where he can download interesting photos for his history project on education in the late 19th century.

8  Michael's interested in fashion history. He would like to know how clothes changed from the late Victorian Age to the early 20th century. He would also like online advice on how to become a costume designer.

9  Selma has to design the scenes of a school play based on Dickens's novels: she wants to find out more about late Victorian architecture and see videos on London in the 19th century.

10  For her project, Chiara has to find out about the greatest inventions of the 19th century. She's fond of machines and would like to share her interest with other people online.

Exam tips
Read all the texts and descriptions first before you try to match them.

Don't just look for the same or similar words in the texts and the descriptions, even if they could be useful. Remember you need to focus on the whole meaning.

Guidance for candidates
A successful strategy to complete this part of the test is to advise candidates to:

- underline what each person is interested in exactly
- read the eight texts to find the necessary information
- underline ANY matches between the people's descriptions and the eight texts
- find the option which matches ALL the things the people are looking for.

A jump into the past

A hardtimes.co.uk

This website has several sections covering life in the Victorian Age. You will be able to learn about social issues such as women's changing role or how children were brought up at the turn of the 19th century. There is also a large photo gallery with hundreds of pictures of typical Victorian schools.

B HallofFame.com

This website will help students to prepare for their exams on English literature in time, from the Middle Ages to the greatest works of the 20th century. You will also find useful mind maps and quizzes about the main novelists and poets of each literary period and what they wrote.

C LadiesandGentlemen.com

Are you a Victorian fashion lover? This website will help you to make your own Victorian dress! Watch the video and follow the step by step guide on how to choose the material and sew your dream costume. You'll look like a character from Dickens's novels in no time.

D londonhistoryweb.co.uk

Did you know that the first underground railway was opened in London in 1863? Find out about this and many other Victorian inventions on this website. You'll find plenty of information on the fantastic machines which were on display at the 1851 Great Exhibition. Users can also share information on the topic in the comment section.

E InventorsWorkshop.com

This website has a lot of amazing information on today's greatest inventions of the 20th century, from the TV to the internet. There is also an interesting section where you can learn about how people used to live before modern era machines like the radio, the telephone and the washing machine were invented.

F 19thcentury.com

This website has lots of key facts, study maps and online tests about the Industrial Revolution and workers in the Victorian Age. You will find out about what it was like to work in a factory in the 19th century and a video on the condition women and children in Victorian factories.

G victoriancloset.co.uk

If you want to learn about what Victorians used to wear, this website has lots of videos and illustrations from 19th-century magazines showing you what was fashionable from the 1850s to the early 1900s. For those who dream to become Victorian dressmakers, there is a section where you can ask for career advice from famous costume designers.

H thevictorianpage.com

This website offers a wide range of material for anyone interested in what London looked like in the Victorian Age. You will be able to look up over 350 illustrations from popular Victorian novels and a 2-hour documentary on schools, factories, houses and many other buildings of the time.

Test 2 Paper 1 Reading

Part 3

Questions 11-15

For each question, choose the correct answer.

Decluttering
13-year-old Tom Trent tell us about his new habits

When Tom Trent started his school project on environmental issues, he had no idea environmental pollution depends on the fact that we all own a lot of things which end up turning into rubbish. Although we don't need many of the things we own, most of us still waste a lot of money on more clothes, devices and objects we could easily live without. This is why he soon decided to make a change and start decluttering his room, which meant getting rid of all the things he hardly used.

He first made a list of all the stuff he never used: he wrote down the clothes which were never worn, and then added his old phones, MP3 players, old notebooks, and a lot of other old things he kept in his drawers and shelves. He also asked his family to do the same and then he started posting pictures of their things online: some of them were for sale, but he gave most of them away for free. It was a great way to avoid producing more rubbish!

Tom now realises that decluttering can help you achieve more than one goal: if you give your things away you will not only help people who can't afford to buy them, but you will also help the environment. In fact, the people using your things won't have to buy new ones. At home, the greatest benefit will be having a lot of extra room. You will find out that when your house is tidier it will take longer for it to become messy again since there are fewer things around. Of course, you must try to avoid buying new things or you'll quickly fill the empty space with stuff again!

Exam tips
First, read the text quickly to find out its general topic. Then read it again carefully and study all the options for each question before choosing the correct one.
Remember that while the first four questions follow the order of the text, the last one is about its global meaning.

Guidance for candidates
In this part candidates need to know the meaning of several adverbs, linking words and idiomatic phrases. Here are a few which appear in the text. Which of the two synonyms on the right is the closest to their meanings?

- although (*line 3*)   unless / even if
- own (*line 3*)   to have / to want
- get rid of (*line 5*)   eliminate / to clean
- hardly (*line 5*)   almost no / difficult
- give away (*line 9*)   throw out / offer as a gift
- for free (*line 9*)   not working / without a payment
- afford (*line 12*)   have enough money / have no interest in
- extra room (*line 14*)   one more room / more space

Paper 1 Reading — Test 2

11 The first paragraph says that

    A people need a lot of clothes and devices to live well.
    B living in today's world is very expensive because you need a lot of things.
    C most of the stuff we have is hardly necessary to live a comfortable life.
    D many people want to have more than they can afford.

12 What is 'decluttering'?

    A giving old things to poor people
    B cleaning and tidying up your home
    C making a list of all the things you rarely use
    D removing things you don't need from your home

13 How did Tom manage to clear most of the things from his home?

    A He sold them to people online.
    B He offered them as gifts.
    C He threw them away.
    D He moved them into an extra room.

14 Which advantage has Tom noticed at home after decluttering?

    A He doesn't have to clean it so often as before.
    B The home is always tidy.
    C It is faster to do the cleaning.
    D There are more rooms in his house.

15 What other benefit might come from decluttering?

    A By selling all the extra things in your home you can earn something and help others save money, too.

    B If you remove all the things you don't need from your home you will help both people and the planet.

    C Decluttering might increase pollution because you throw away a lot of old things when you clear your home.

    D When you get rid of your old things you will have more space to fill with all the new things you will buy.

Test 2 — Paper 1 Reading

Part 4

Questions 16-20

Five sentences have been removed from the text below.
For each space, choose the correct answer.
There are three extra sentences which you do not need to use.

How the violin changed my life
by Sam Reynolds, 26

I was born into a family of doctors, so my parents were really surprised when I told them I wanted to be a violinist. At first, they thought it was just a temporary thing, since children often dream to do unusual jobs but they quickly change their mind when they grow up. **16**

Learning the violin is not a piece of cake: it means practising for hours every day, pain in your fingertips and neck, and a lot of disappointment. Most of the time, especially at the beginning, it sounds bad. **17**

Anyway, I kept taking classes and practising, until I joined an ensemble and that's when the fun started. **18** When you eventually perform in front of an audience, the joy you give to others with your music will make the whole effort worthwhile. **19**

When I teach my students I always tell them I remember what it feels like when you can't join in with your friends because you have to practise, so I often tell them about my childhood years.

I have never regretted being a musician. **20** She often jokes that I would be a terrible doctor, but in the end my job is not so different to hers: she cures people's bodies, but I cure their souls.

Guidance for candidates
This part of the reading paper is to test candidates' ability to follow the narrative of a text and understand its structure. In particular, candidates need to:

- refer to the sentences both before and after the gap
- make sure that the sentence they select matches grammatically
- then check that the whole text surrounding the selected sentence make sense.

Paper 1 Reading — Test 2

A I realised playing with other musicians is one of the most thrilling experiences you can have.

B My sister, who is a doctor, agrees that it was the best choice.

C So after a few years I stopped taking lessons and took up the guitar.

D This is why, during the first few years, I thought of giving up.

E She doesn't understand why I chose this job instead of being a doctor.

F The violin is not as difficult to learn as you may think, though.

G When I told them again three years later, however, they realised I was serious about my decision.

H I also tell them I know what it takes to fight against those 4 strings and make them sound pleasant.

Exam tips
Once you've chosen the right option, ask yourself why the other ones aren't acceptable.
For example, try and answer questions such as:

- Does any part of the text mention a thrilling experience?
- Does the text mention the writer's sister in any paragraph?
- Is there any further information about guitar lessons?
- Are there any negative words suggesting the writer was unhappy about his results?
- Focus on the tense of the verb: does it fit in with the rest of any paragraph?
- Does the writer explain why the violin isn't very difficult in any paragraph?
- Do the pronouns 'them' and 'they' refer to anyone in particular?
- Does the writer say anything else about what he has learnt from his experience?

Test 2 Paper 1 Reading

Part 5

Questions 21-26

For each question, choose the correct answer.

The healthy diet of Italians

Contrary to what most people would think, Italians are **(21)** _____ slimmer and healthier than Americans despite their love of eating. What is their secret? A recent research study **(22)** _____ only 9% of Italians weigh too much compared to over 30% of Americans, but many American eat Italian food in the US. **(23)** _____, the Italian food people eat in the US is hardly the same food we find in Italy. First of all, in Italy pasta is never considered a whole meal. Instead, you should have it as a small first **(24)** _____ at lunch and dinner, followed by fresh vegetables.

Another difference is that American plates of Italian food are far bigger than the ones served in Italy. Italians do eat meatballs and lasagna, but on weekdays pasta dishes are served in a light sauce with herbs or a small **(25)** _____ of meat. Moreover, in Italy, a portion of pasta is half the size Americans normally eat, because Italians want to leave **(26)** _____ in their stomach for whatever is going to be served after the first course.

21	**A** more	**B** much	**C** not	**D** many
22	**A** tells	**B** declares	**C** advises	**D** reports
23	**A** Instead	**B** So	**C** However	**D** Though
24	**A** course	**B** plate	**C** dish	**D** food
25	**A** number	**B** lot	**C** amount	**D** size
26	**A** room	**B** spaces	**C** area	**D** enough

Exam tips
Reading Part 5 is designed to test not only vocabulary but also elements of grammar knowledge, so you should try and focus on each gap and answer questions like these:

21 Which two words cannot be used before a comparative adjective?
22 Which verb best describes what a research study does?
23 Which of these linking words is usually followed by a comma?
24 Which of the four words is the first 'part of a meal'?
25 Which word can be used with 'small' and 'meat', which is uncountable?
26 Which of these words means the same as 'space'?

Paper 1 Reading — Test 2

Part 6

Questions 27-32

For each question, write the correct answer.
Write **one** word for each gap.

How to Become a Teenage Video Game Tester

If you are keen **(27)** _____ video games, game testing is the perfect way to enjoy **(28)** _____ and earn extra pocket money as well. A game tester plays games to check if they work well before they are sold to the public. Every game you test is a similar version to the **(29)** _____ people will buy and play in the future.

As a game tester, you must play the game many times to find out if there are **(30)** _____ issues. However, you will also have to go through all the menus, settings, etc. to **(31)** _____ sure there are no bugs and they work correctly.

To check the whole game you will also need to perform every move a player could possibly perform while playing the game. It will take a long time to complete each part, but you probably won't mind **(32)** _____ this job as you love playing, will you?

Exam tips
First, read the whole text quickly to find out its general topic.
When you choose a word, check if it makes sense with the words that come before and after the gap.
After you've chosen the correct words, read the whole text to make sure it makes sense, carefully checking your spelling.

Guidance for candidates
To help complete this part successfully, candidates could be given an exercise testing their knowledge of grammar elements.
In this case, they could be given an exercise like this:

What kind of words is missing from each gap?

| quantifier | preposition | reflexive pronoun | verb (x2) | indefinite pronoun |

27 _____   30 _____
28 _____   31 _____
29 _____   32 _____

Test 2 Paper 2 Writing

Part 1

You **must** answer this question.
Write your answers in about **100 words** on the answer sheet.

Question 1

Read this email from your English cousin and the notes you have made.

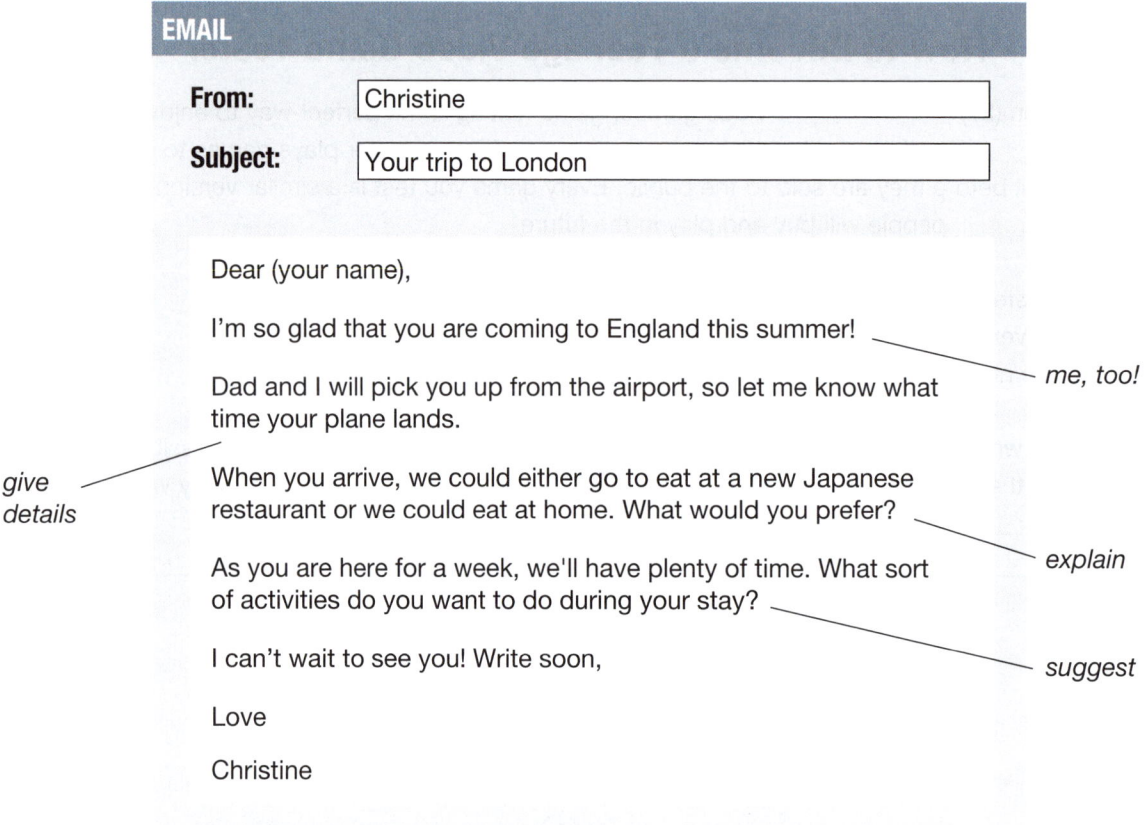

Write your **email** to your English cousin using **all the notes**.

Exam tips
In Writing Part 1, you have to express your opinion, agree or disagree, or give advice or suggestions.
Remember to address every prompt of the email, in the given order.
You could do this using different words (synonyms) than the ones on the paper.

Guidance for candidates
To help candidates develop a series of synonyms apt to reply to an email, they could be given short exercises like this one:

Which expression can you use in the first paragraph instead of 'too'?
A ☐ as well   B ☐ alike   C ☐ even
Which verb can you use instead of 'land'?
A ☐ go   B ☐ arrive   C ☐ reach
Which word do you have to use when you explain the reason for something?
A ☐ although   B ☐ however   C ☐ because
Which phrase can you use to cover the fourth note?
A ☐ how about   B ☐ do you mind   C ☐ would you like

Paper 2 Writing — Test 2

Part 2

Choose **one** of these questions.
Write your answers in about **100 words** on the answer sheet.

Question 2

You see this advertisement on a website.

COMPUTER GAMES
Do you enjoy playing computer games?
Which is your favourite one?
What do you like about it?
Write an article answering these questions and we will publish the next one in next month's issue.

Write your **article**.

Question 3

Your English teacher has asked you to write a story.
Your story must begin with this sentence.

> *I sat on the bus with the kitten in my arms, wondering how to convince Mum and Dad to keep him.*

Write your **story**.

Exam tips
Plan your **story** before writing. Imagine being the hero of the story. Make a list of things you could say or do to convince your parents to keep the kitten.

Guidance for candidates
In Writing Part 3 candidates are asked to write a **story**. They should remember to:

- plan how to start, develop and finish the story
- think of the vocabulary they need to tell the story
- avoid general adjectives like good, nice, bad
- use a range of past tenses, in particular: past simple, past perfect and past continuous
- use suitable time expressions (*suddenly, while, then, as soon as, later*, etc.).

Test 2 Paper 3 Listening

Part 1

 Questions 1-7

For each question, choose the correct answer.

---

1 How did the boy get to the appointment?

A ☐

B ☐

C ☐

2 What time are they leaving for the concert?

A ☐

B ☐

C ☐

3 What's Mark doing this weekend?

A ☐

B ☐

C ☐

Exam tips
Before listening to the recording think of the words to describe what you can see in the pictures to prepare for the answer.

Guidance for candidates
In Listening Part 1 candidates are asked to listen to short dialogues to answer the questions. They should focus on the pictures and, before choosing the correct ones, answer to questions such as:

1 What are the three means of transport in the pictures?
2 What time is it in each Licture?
3 What are the people doing in each picture?
4 Where are the people in the pictures?
5 Which places are in the pictures?
6 Which food is in each picture?
7 What's the weather like in each picture?

Paper 3 Listening Test 2

4 Which photograph are they going to send?

 A ☐
 B ☐
 C ☐

5 Where is the boy going on holiday?

 A ☐
 B ☐
 C ☐

6 What did Tracy forget to buy?

 A ☐
 B ☐
 C ☐

7 What will the weather be like on Thursday?

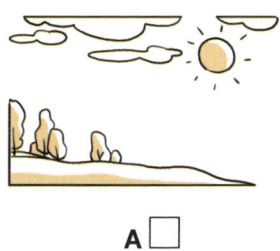 A ☐
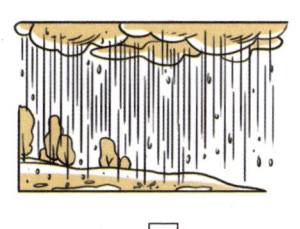 B ☐
 C ☐

Test 2 Paper 3 Listening

Part 2

 Questions 8-13

For each question, choose the correct answer.

8 You will hear two students talking about a new teacher: what does he look like?
   A his hair's curly
   B he has no hair
   C he wears glasses

9 You will hear a boy asking his grandmother about her childhood. What does she regret about that time?
   A the meat she rarely ate
   B one of her grandmother's dishes
   C boiled beef and cabbage

10 You will hear a conversation between a girl and her father: what are they talking about?
   A a bus card
   B a remote control
   C a schoolbag

11 You will hear a teacher talking to her students about a school trip: what does she recommend?
   A visiting a monument
   B buying something at the shop
   C looking for souvenirs at the market

12 You will hear a girl asking for directions. Where does she want to go?
   A the railway station
   B the park
   C the bus station

13 You will hear two teenagers talking about a lesson: how does the boy feel about the topic of the lesson?
   A annoyed
   B very worried
   C interested

Exam tips
If you don't know the meaning of a word you hear in the dialogue or read in the question, try to guess its meaning from the context.

Guidance for candidates
In this part of the test at least two of the options are mentioned, but candidates must pay attention to the whole conversation to understand which option is correct.
During the first listening they should concentrate on the general gist of each dialogue to choose the correct answer. They should use the second listening to check their chosen answer.

Paper 3 Listening — Test 2

Part 3

 Questions 14-19

For each question, write the correct answer in the gap.
Write **one** or **two words** or a **number** or a **date** or a **time**.

You will hear a teacher telling his students about a school trip.

Weekend hike in the country

Saturday
departure time: at (**14**) _____ a.m. from school

what students must bring:
  * no more than one (**15**) _____
  * a sleeping bag
  * warm clothes and swimming things
  * (**16**) £ _____ for food, drinks

Sunday
morning until midday: hike and lunch at the lake

afternoon:
  * bus stop (**17**) _____ the campsite
  * journey to Leavenworth 30 minutes
  * remember to bring (**18**) _____ and call
    (**19**) _____ in case of emergency

Exam tips
Remember that in Listening Part 3, you must fill the gaps for missing information while you listen to it. It's very important you read the text first, so you can think of what kind of word to expect (a time, a price, a day, etc).

Guidance for candidates
Candidates should try to work out what kind of word to expect for each gap before they listen to the text. For example, they could answer questions like these:

For each gap, what word do you expect?
14 a time / a place
15 an object / a person
16 a container / a sum of money
17 an adverb / a preposition
18 a noun / an adjective
19 an email address / a number

Test 2 — Paper 3 Listening

Part 4

 Questions 20-25

For each question, choose the correct answer.

You will hear an interview with a teenage fashion blogger called Erika Mendel.

20 Which of these figures are more important in today's fashion trends?
- **A** journalists, stylists and celebrities
- **B** bloggers, influencers and editors
- **C** both of these groups

21 Erika says that all fashion bloggers
- **A** post fashion photos on their websites.
- **B** communicate their personal tastes in fashion.
- **C** write about their favourite fashion trends.

22 Fashion bloggers may become less popular because of competition from
- **A** social media.
- **B** fashion influencers.
- **C** more successful bloggers.

23 What do fashion bloggers have?
- **A** their own website
- **B** an account on social media
- **C** a personal fashion company

24 What is an influencer's success based on?
- **A** the age of his or her followers
- **B** the clothes he or she wears in their posts
- **C** how old he or she is

25 An editor's job is to
- **A** sit in the front row of fashion shows.
- **B** launch their own fashion brand.
- **C** advertise a magazine's ideas on fashion.

Exam tips
While you read the questions before listening, try to understand the context and the people acting in it.

Guidance for candidates
Candidates could find it useful to think about words related to the topic of the interview. Exercises like the following one could be useful.
This interview will be about fashion bloggers. Which words do you expect to find? Circle the words in the list below.

disappointing	business	magazine	drawing	boring	well-known	celebrity
vegetables	relax	exam	fare	blanket	research	advertising	scientific
trendy	success	hall	readers	court	viewers	sleeves	spoon	social media

Paper 4 Speaking — Test 2

Part 1 (2-3 minutes)

Phase 1

The interlocutor asks the same questions to candidate A and candidate B.

Interlocutor Good morning.
Can I have your mark sheets, please?
I'm (*interlocutor's name*) and this is (*assessor's name*).

What's your name?
How old are you?

Back-up Prompts

Where do you come from?   Do you live in *name of town/city/region*?
Are you a student?   Do you study?
What do you study?   What subject do you study?

Thank you.

Phase 2

The interlocutor asks some personal questions to each candidate.
Ask Candidate A first.

Back-up Prompts

Interlocutor **Candidate A**
How do you usually travel to school?   Do you usually travel by bus/train?
Can you tell us about your hometown?   Tell us about your hometown: is it small/big?

Candidate B
Can you describe your house or flat?   Do you live in a house or a flat?
What did you do last weekend?   Did you do anything last weekend? What?

Thank you.

Exam tips
In Speaking Part 1 – Phase 2 you are expected to give answers to questions about your personal life, tastes, routines. Listen carefully to the question and remember that these answers must be a little longer than in Phase 1.

Guidance for candidates
Candidates are often nervous in the first stages of Speaking and make mistakes with accuracy. They can practise speaking with ease about familiar topics, avoiding common mistakes. An exercise like this could be useful.

Find the mistakes in each of these answers.
1 I travel to school by foot but sometimes I go with the train.
2 Is near the sea and there are a big harbour.
3 My house is on the fourth floor and is such big.
4 Last weekend I go in the centre with my friend.

Candidates should not worry about not understanding everything immediately. If a candidate is struggling with an answer, then the examiner will use a rephrased question to help them.

Test 2 Paper 4 Speaking

Part 2 (2-3 minutes)

The interlocutor gives each candidate a photograph with a different topic.

Interlocutor Now I'd like each of you to talk on your own about something. I'm going to give each of you a photograph and I'd like you to talk about it.
A, here is your photograph. It shows **people in a shop**.
B, you just listen.
A, please tell us what you can see in the photograph.

A

Back-up prompts
- Talk about the people/person.
- Talk about the place.
- Talk about other things in the photograph.

Interlocutor Thank you.

Interlocutor B, here is your photograph. It shows **people at a party**.
A, you just listen.
B, please tell us what you can see in the photograph.

B

Back-up prompts
- Talk about the people/person.
- Talk about the place.
- Talk about other things in the photograph.

Interlocutor Thank you.

Exam tips
When you describe photos with people, focus on what they are doing and if they look happy, sad, etc. Learn these simple, but useful action verbs:
they are standing / they are sitting / they are lying / they are running / they are holding hands / they are smiling

Use prepositions of place to say where the objects in the picture are.

Paper 4 Speaking — Test 2

Part 3 (2-3 minutes)

Interlocutor Now, in this part of the test you're going to talk about something together for about two minutes. I'm going to describe a situation to you.

You want to go camping by the sea with a group of friends. You are planning what to pack in your bags. Here are some things you could take along. Talk together and say which thing would be the most useful.

All right? Now, talk together.

Part 4 (3 minutes)

The interlocutor asks questions related to what candidates discussed in Part 3.

Interlocutor Do you like camping or do you prefer other types of holiday? Why?
Where do you like going on holiday?
What is the best time to go on holiday?
Do you enjoy going on holiday with your friends or your family?
Do you like travelling abroad?

Thank you. That is the end of the test.

Select any of the following prompts, as appropriate:
- **How/What about you?**
- **Do you agree?**
- **What do you think?**

Test 3   Paper 1 Reading

Part 1

Questions 1-5

For each question, choose the correct answer.

1

DO NOT LEAVE WITHOUT ASKING THE TUTOR

A Speak to the tutor before leaving.

B The tutor will leave with you.

C The tutor asks to be left alone.

2

PLEASE WAIT HERE TO BE SEATED

A You may sit here while you wait.

B The waiter will take you to your place.

C The waiter will move the seats.

3

Jane called. Said she would call again after 7 this evening.

A You should call Jane after 7 p.m.

B Jane promised to call this evening.

C Jane will telephone around 6 p.m.

44

4

A Mike should use the scarf since it's cold.

B Mike should bring the scarf with him.

C Mike can keep the scarf for tonight.

5

MAY CONTAIN MILK PRODUCTS AND NUTS

A Nuts are present in this food.

B There are no nuts in this food.

C It is possible to find nuts in this food.

Test 3 Paper 1 Reading

Part 2

Questions 6-10

For each question, choose the correct answer.

The people below are all looking for a magazine to buy.
On the opposite page there are descriptions of eight magazines.
Decide which magazine would be the most suitable for the people below.

6

Peter likes cycling and hillwalking, but what he really loves is finding out about the latest trends – technology, fast cars and music. He lives for the future and really isn't interested in finding out about the past.

7

Shula is very sociable and likes meeting new people. She's into fashion and makes her own clothes as a hobby in her free time.

8

Kieran would like to be help a local charity but isn't sure what to do. He's a vegetarian and interested in the environment. He's still at school so he isn't looking for a job at the moment.

9

Jessica loves art in all its forms and really enjoys being outdoors. One day, she hopes to join a theatre group that performs in the open air. Her problem is finding people who are interested in the same thing.

10

Sonia has lots of hobbies. Her favourite way to spend time is going to the mountains and hillwalking, but as her family lives in a city, that's not always possible. Whatever the weather, you can be sure to find her busy and happy, even if it's at home.

Our Newsstand

A OUTDOORS!

A great new magazine for anyone who likes to get out and be active, come rain or shine. Lots of ideas and advice on camping, climbing, as well as things you can do in your own house and garden.

B TOP ACT

A magazine for young fans of the theatre. We let you know what's on near you, from classic and traditional plays to modern and interesting productions. You can also find a youth theatre group near you on our local contacts page.

C PLANET A

Take a look at our free monthly newsletter, printed on 100% recycled paper. It's full of work opportunities for those young people who have left school and want to protect our planet. Don't miss the chance to help and earn some money, while learning the latest trends about ecology.

D THE LATEST

There's nothing old-fashioned about our magazine! Each week, we have a different focus on the latest developments in the world of either science, fashion, theatre or music. If something new is happening, you'll know about it here first!

E YOUTH NEWS BRIEF

In a few pages you can get all the latest facts you need about the world we live in. Illustrated with maps and diagrams, charts and tables, Youth News Brief gives you the news that young people want to read!

F COUNTRY EXPLORER

A magazine for those who love nature and the countryside. This magazine gives you information to help you plan your adventures in the wild. We also organise trips for small groups, so come along and make new friends! Forget your boring town life and experience the beautiful countryside with our help.

G GO DO IT!

Do you have big ideas for saving the planet? Do you want to stop climate change? Would you like to be part of a project with other young people that can make a difference? At last, here's the magazine that tells you how to find a local group and how to get involved.

H HUMAN TOUCH

If you want to get in touch with people like you, and to read about the latest styles and trends, then this is your new monthly. We have everything from knitting and sewing patterns to our letters page, from news on technology to techno!

Part 3

Questions 11-15

For each question, choose the correct answer.

The Way to do Science
14-year-old Jim Doherty tells us the secret to be a good scientist

Whenever you want to know the right way to do something, it's always best to ask an expert. So last week I met with Doctor Watson, a successful scientist who has recently published a book on how to be a good scientist. As I would love to go to university to study science when I'm older, I was really interested to hear what he had to say. Here I'll try to give you his most useful advice.

First, and most important of all, never do things that bore you. If you're really interested in what you're doing, you'll probably produce valuable results, but if you're not, you will only waste your time, and probably discover nothing new at all.

Next, and rather strangely, Watson says you should always try to work with people who are cleverer than you are. 'It's a bit like learning to play tennis,' he says, 'you know you only really get better when you're playing someone who makes you work harder and try to reach that higher level.'

It sounds like hard work to me!

Thirdly, you have to be ready to take risks. You can't stay in the 'safety zone' all the time, feeling comfortable and knowing all the answers. Instead, science is about the difficult questions we haven't answered yet, and it's also about making some mistakes.

Last, and this is Watson's secret, you must always be willing to let others examine your work and ideas and listen to their views and opinions. Of course, you don't have to agree with every opinion you hear, but informed judgement from other scientists is the best way to check your work is correct and of value. If other experts approve of your work, it will make you more confident, and their doubts will certainly help your thinking.

By the time I left our meeting, I was beginning to see myself as another Galileo or Einstein. Of course, that's foolish, but I'm sure they would agree with the rules for science I had learnt from Dr Watson!

Paper 1 Reading — Test 3

11 The writer met with Dr Watson to

    A give him some advice.
    B write a book about him.
    C find out how to be a good scientist.
    D get a job as a scientist.

12 Watson believes that if you are not interested in your subject

    A other people will see that you are bored.
    B you will not be able to persuade people to help you.
    C people will think you are wasting their time.
    D your discoveries will look old and out of date.

13 Watson says that a scientist should

    A only spend time with intelligent people.
    B use sport to get to a higher level of work.
    C avoid taking too many risks.
    D not be worried about making mistakes.

14 According to Dr Watson, other scientists' opinions

    A can help you check your work is correct.
    B will make you less confident.
    C are always correct.
    D will make you doubt their work.

15 Which of the following best describes the writer of this article?

A A curious young scientist who is keen to learn.	**C** A scientist who dreams of success instead of working for it.
B A friendly writer who is happy to share what he learns.	**D** A writer who believes we have to work hard to understand science.

Part 4

Questions 16-20

Five sentences have been removed from the text below.
For each space, choose the correct answer.
There are three extra sentences which you do not need to use.

Gap Years

Have you decided what you want to do when you finish school? Do you think you'll go to university? Today, having a gap year is something that many students do between leaving school and starting university. **16** But a gap year can also be great for opening your mind, building your character and finding out about the world.

Many students use the gap year as a chance to travel around the world on a long holiday. **17** But the idea is really to use this time to learn new skills and have new experiences before university, so lots of young people prefer to do something useful to help others. **18** Companies like Raleigh International organise projects like this in different parts of the world, such as South America or Africa. Participants help local people and in return they learn a lot about themselves and develop new skills which are useful for their future.

Of course, if you are planning to have a gap year, you'll need money. **19** Many do evening and weekend jobs while they are still at school in order to finance their gap year. Some also find jobs in the different countries they visit while they are on the gap year, but you need to find out about if you'll be allowed to work in each country before you leave home. For example, in many places you may need a special work permit. **20** You won't want any unexpected surprises when you arrive at a border!

Paper 1 Reading — Test 3

A For example, many work as volunteers on social or environmental projects.

B You will also need to find out if you need to get a visa for any of the countries you plan to visit.

C But there are lots of difficulties related to gap years, too.

D After finishing school, it can be lots of fun to take time off before going back to studying.

E Student's parents always pay for the gap year.

F Saving enough can be difficult, so most people work for a period before travelling.

G You can do a gap year before going to university.

H They want to see new places and meet new people.

Test 3 Paper 1 Reading

Part 5

Questions 21-26

For each question, choose the correct answer.

Man's Best Friend

Scientific research suggests that having a pet at home is good for your health. We've known for centuries that a dog will **(21)** _____ leave you, and will stay by your side in good times and bad, but **(22)** _____ is new is our understanding of the health benefits pets can bring to us.

Cats, dogs and even canaries can **(23)** _____ you feel good. Detailed research has shown that the presence of a pet can alter our moods and **(24)** _____ stress. We like to have a companion when we arrive home late **(25)** _____ night, who greets us with great affection, and a few barks or miaows from our pet **(26)** _____ us know we're not alone.

In fact, if we think about it, it's not surprising that pets prolong our lives: they give us so much extra pleasure and happiness, it can only be good for us.

21	**A** never	**B** always	**C** sometimes	**D** often
22	**A** that	**B** what	**C** how	**D** which
23	**A** make	**B** give	**C** do	**D** offer
24	**A** reduce	**B** subtract	**C** change	**D** decline
25	**A** before	**B** after	**C** at	**D** in
26	**A** make	**B** let	**C** tell	**D** want

Part 6

Questions 27-32

For each question, write the correct answer.
Write **one** word for each gap.

Loftwood Sports Centre

Are you interested (**27**) _____ learning a new sport? Come to our friendly sports centre and learn with our team of qualified instructors. There are courses for people of (**28**) _____ ages, from children to teenagers, adults and pensioners. We offer courses in volleyball, netball, badminton, archery and judo as well (**29**) _____ many others. In the summer we can also teach you tennis and athletics.

All our courses (**30**) _____ for 16 weeks, with two lessons every week. There are extra activities and competitions at the weekend for anyone (**31**) _____ is interested. There is a maximum of 20 people on each course, but one-to-one lessons are also available.

Our sports centre is extremely bright and clean with all the (**32**) _____ modern equipment, and there is a large car park.

Call us on 374 8921 for more information!

Test 3 Paper 2 Writing

Part 1

You **must** answer this question.
Write your answers in about **100 words** on the answer sheet.

Question 1

Read this email from your uncle George (your mother's brother) and the notes you have made.

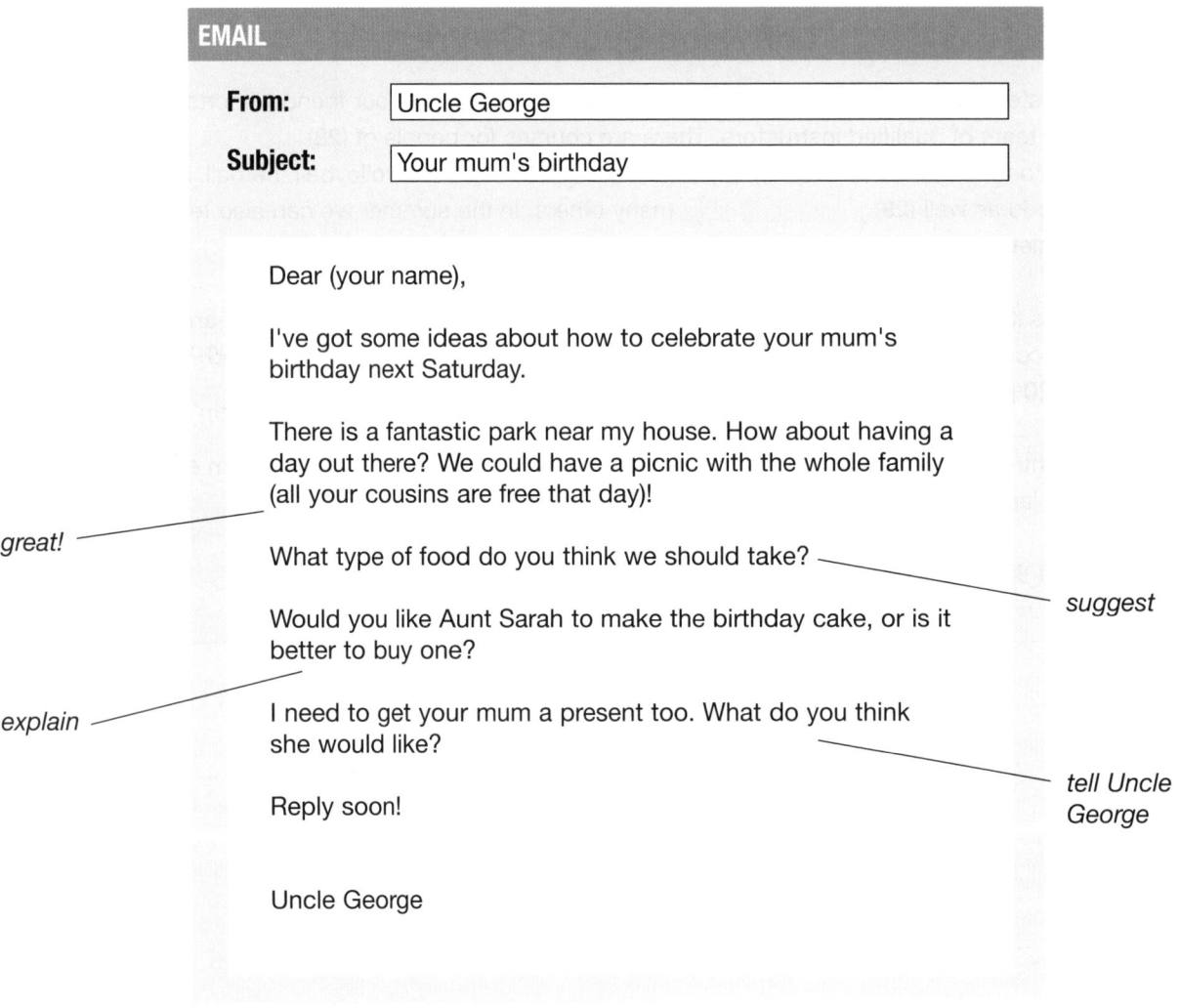

Write your **email** to your uncle George using **all the notes**.

Paper 2 Writing — Test 3

Part 2

Choose **one** of these questions.
Write your answer in about **100 words** on the answer sheet.

Question 2

You see this announcement on the school notice board.

> **Articles wanted!**
> **What's your favourite possession?**
>
> Write an article describing your favourite possession.
> When did you get it? Was it a present?
> Why is it special to you?
> The best article we receive will win a prize of £5!

Write your **article**.

Question 3

Your class is collecting stories in English for a book that will be sold locally.
Your story must begin with this sentence.

> *It was the most dangerous game they had ever played.*

Write your **story**.

Test 3 Paper 3 Listening

Part 1

 Questions 1-7

For each question, choose the correct answer.

1 Where did she leave the keys?

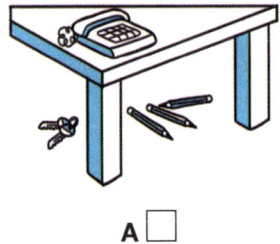

A ☐

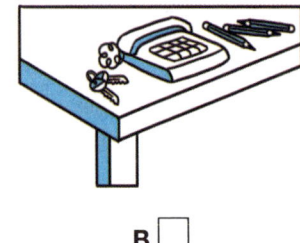

B ☐

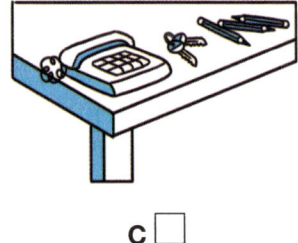

C ☐

2 How did she get to school?

A ☐

B ☐

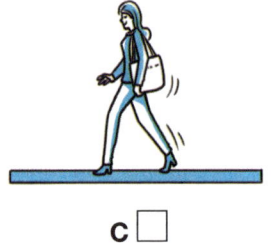

C ☐

3 Where is the supermarket?

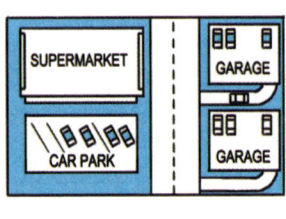

A ☐

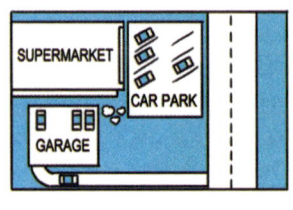

B ☐

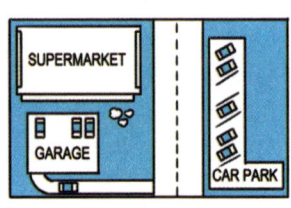

C ☐

Paper 3 Listening — **Test 3**

4 What was the weather like yesterday?

A ☐

B ☐

C ☐

5 What are they going to give their daughter?

A ☐

B ☐

C ☐

6 What date is her aunt coming?

A ☐

B ☐

C ☐

7 What ingredients does the boy need to get?

A ☐

B ☐

C ☐

Test 3 Paper 3 Listening

Part 2

 Questions 8-13

For each question, choose the correct answer.

8 You will hear two friends talking about the boy's 18th birthday. What present are his parents probably going to give him?
   A a bicycle
   B a digital camera
   C a holiday

9 You will hear two people talking about a flight. What time will the plane leave?
   A 12.30
   B 1.15
   C 4.30

10 You will hear two friends talking about a party. What did the boy like best?
   A the music
   B the food
   C the people

11 You will hear a girl buying a train ticket. Which type of ticket does she buy?
   A a single
   B a fixed return
   C an open return

12 You will hear a conversation in a clothes shop. What's wrong with the first top the assistant shows the girl?
   A the colour
   B the size
   C the style

13 You will hear two friends talking about homework. Why doesn't the girl help the boy?
   A She's too busy.
   B She thinks he's lazy.
   C She can't understand the exercises.

Paper 3 Listening — Test 3

Part 3

 Questions 14-19

For each question, write the correct answer in the gap.
Write **one** or **two words** or a **number** or a **date** or a **time**.

You will hear a man talking about a country fair.

The Country Show and Fair

The show...

Opens at 9 o'clock and closes at **(14)** _____.

The hand-made products are cheapest in the **(15)** _____ section of the showground.

The colour of the all-day ticket is **(16)** _____ and the price is **(17)** _____.

The fruit and vegetable competition is in the tent in the **(18)** _____ of the showground.

The traditional sports are usually more than **(19)** _____ hours long.

Test 3 Paper 3 Listening

Part 4

 Questions 20-25

For each question, choose the correct answer.

You will hear an interview with a TV hostess talking on the radio about her programme.

20 One reason why the interviewer likes Katie's show is that
   A   he is a skilled cook.
   B   he loves good food.
   C   it taught him how to boil water.

21 Katie thinks that
   A   some people don't cook because they worry about the result being bad.
   B   people who watch her programme often go out to restaurants.
   C   good food takes a long time to prepare.

22 The interviewer
   A   buys frozen dinners every day.
   B   has trouble finding time to go to the supermarket.
   C   goes shopping for cooking ingredients once a week.

23 Katie says that people who don't have time for shopping every day
   A   buy some amazing things to keep in their kitchens.
   B   should buy frozen dinners and cans of beans.
   C   can make a variety of dishes if they know what to buy.

24 Katie doesn't think that
   A   good cooks use expensive knives, pots and pans.
   B   her mother was a good cook.
   C   expensive kitchen equipment is necessary.

25 What advice does Katie give the interviewer?
   A   He should stop thinking of reasons why he can't cook.
   B   He should cook and eat natural food.
   C   He should take the opportunity to make mistakes.

Paper 4 Speaking — Test 3

Part 1 (2-3 minutes)

Phase 1

The interlocutor asks the same questions to candidate A and candidate B.

Interlocutor Good afternoon.
Can I have your mark sheets, please?
I'm (*interlocutor's name*) and this is (*assessor's name*).

What's your name?
How old are you?

Back-up Prompts

Where do you come from?   Do you live in *name of town/city/region*?
Are you a student?   Do you study?
What do you study?   What subject do you study?

Thank you.

Phase 2

The interlocutor asks some personal questions to each candidate.
Ask Candidate A first.

Back-up Prompts

Interlocutor **Candidate A**
Tell us about the people you live with.   Do you live with your family?
What kind of music do you enjoy listening to?   Do you like listening to music? Why?

Candidate B
Tell us about your English teacher.   What's your English teacher like?
What do you enjoy doing in your free time?   What do you do in your free time?

Thank you.

Test 3 Paper 4 Speaking

Part 2 (2-3 minutes)

The interlocutor gives each candidate a photograph with a different topic.

Interlocutor Now I'd like each of you to talk on your own about something. I'm going to give each of you a photograph and I'd like you to talk about it.
  A, here is your photograph. It shows **a family doing something together**.
  B, you just listen.
  A, please tell us what you can see in the photograph.

A

Back-up prompts
- Talk about the people/person.
- Talk about the place.
- Talk about other things in the photograph.

Interlocutor Thank you.

Interlocutor **B**, here is your photograph. It shows **two people walking**.
  A, you just listen.
  B, please tell us what you can see in the photograph.

B

Back-up prompts
- Talk about the people/person.
- Talk about the place.
- Talk about other things in the photograph.

Interlocutor Thank you.

Paper 4 Speaking — Test 3

Part 3 (2-3 minutes)

Interlocutor Now, in this part of the test you're going to talk about something together for about two minutes. I'm going to describe a situation to you.

**Your grandfather is coming to visit you this summer. Talk together about the different places you could take him, and decide which two would be best for him.
Here is a picture with some ideas to help you.**

All right? Now, talk together.

Part 4 (3 minutes)

The interlocutor asks questions related to what candidates discussed in Part 3.

Interlocutor Which places do you usually take relatives to when they visit?
Which places near where you live are best for children?
Why?
Which are best for old people? Why?
What places (like parks, museums, stadiums and so on) do you like or dislike visiting?
What do you think is the best time of year to visit a city? Why?

Thank you. That is the end of the test.

Select any of the following prompts, as appropriate:
- **How/What about you?**
- **Do you agree?**
- **What do you think?**

Test 4 Paper 1 Reading

Part 1

Questions 1-5

For each question, choose the correct answer.

1

> **Library Reading Rooms**
> please put mobile phones on silent at all times

A You must turn off your mobile phone before you get into the library.

B Mobile phones are not allowed in the reading rooms.

C Keep your mobile phones quiet when you are in the library.

2

> Kay, your tennis coach rang to ask if you can put off the lesson to Saturday. Text him if you can't.
> Dad

What did Kay's tennis coach do?

A He rang to cancel the lesson on Saturday.

B He called to change their lesson.

C He texted to confirm the Saturday lesson.

3

> If red light shows, your snack is unavailable. Please, select another one.

A Wait until the red light shows to choose a snack.

B Choose a different drink if the red light is on.

C If the red light is on, the machine is out of order.

64

Paper 1 Reading — Test 4

4

Changing Rooms
Any personal item
left in the lockers
after 7 p.m.
will be removed overnight

A You may not find a thing if you left it in the locker yesterday.

B People's items in the lockers are stolen after 7 p.m.

C You must remove your items from lockers by 7 p.m.

5

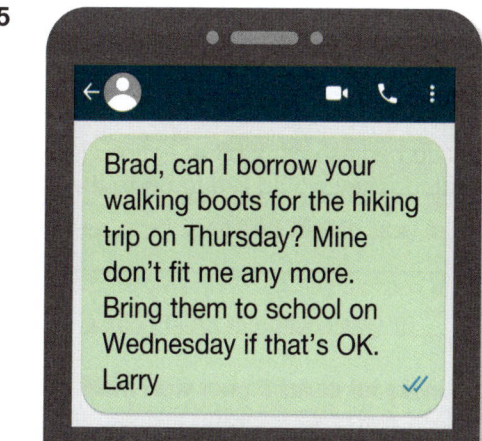

Brad, can I borrow your walking boots for the hiking trip on Thursday? Mine don't fit me any more. Bring them to school on Wednesday if that's OK.
Larry

A Larry hasn't got suitable equipment for the hiking trip.

B Brad must buy Larry a pair of walking boots by Thursday.

C Larry wants to lend Brad his boots on Wednesday.

Part 2

Questions 6-10

For each question, choose the correct answer.

The people below all want to go to the cinema.
On the opposite page there are descriptions of eight films.
Decide which film would be the most suitable for the people below.

6  Ryan is fond of science fiction. He really loves stories set in a future world run by robots or adventures in distant parts of the universe. He would prefer to book an early afternoon ticket online.

7  Emma and her sister Roberta enjoy comedies with a bit of action. They prefer films with an unexpected ending. They would like to go to the cinema after dinner.

8  Sharon and her father would like to go to the cinema together. She enjoys films about people her age, but her father usually finds them boring. They both like adventure movies with a lot of visual effects.

9  Ian and his classmates would like to organise a morning trip to the cinema to see a film based on the real life of a famous writer. They need to book in advance and possibly get a student discount.

10  Elizabeth and Margaret are keen on thrillers. They would like to see a film about a mystery. They would like to go in the evening, as they are both at school until 5.30 p.m.

Paper 1 Reading — Test 4

Latest movies out now

A The Odeon: The man you will be

In 2050, a spaceship on a mission to Mars goes missing under mysterious circumstances. Mark Riverdale leaves Earth in search of it and finds out something incredible. If you enjoy stories about time travel this is the film for you. Book online at www.theodeon.co.uk. Shows from 6.30 p.m. to 11.30 p.m.

B Movieplex West: Have we met before?

Because of a mistake a famous actor who has just died is sent back to Earth as a hairdresser. When he finds out his ex-girlfriend is a regular customer, he learns about her real feelings for him. This is the ideal choice if you love laughing and enjoy movies with the final surprise. Showtimes: 3.00 p.m. - 5.00 p.m. - 7.00 p.m. - 9.00 p.m.

C Lumière's Hall: The man who loved poetry

After three women disappear, Detective Marlowe receives a poem from someone who signs himself William Shakespeare: it contains clues for the police to find the missing women. Will Marlowe manage to solve the case? Get ready for a lot of twists and turns. Shows from 2.15 p.m. to 10.30 p.m.

D Ariston Movie Theatre: Too good to be true

In 2055 Herman and his family move to New Arcadia. Computers have replaced the government and everything is perfect. What they don't know is that one person in their family is a robot, too. Morning to evening shows starting from 8.30 a.m. until 6.30 p.m. Book in advance on www.aristmov.com.

E Cineapolis: The mysteries of the Arctic Sea

Discover the North Pole's hidden underwater treasures with this marine wildlife documentary. Morning shows available for school groups at a discount. For information and bookings send an inquiry to ed.dyson@cineapolis.com.

F The Blockbuster: The picture of Oscar Wilde

This biographic film will take you back to the late Victorian Age to discover on the life of Oscar Wilde, the famous writer of plays and poetry. Morning screening for groups of more than 8 people can be arranged. Write to tpoow@blockb.com for information or to book. Tickets for school and university students are 50% off.

G Kineworld: Who's that boy?

A new boy has come to Anna's high school: he's great fun and popular, but nobody knows anything about his life outside school. When Anna discovers his secret, an incredible adventure starts. Enjoy this movie that combines comedy, teen romance and aliens in 3D. Pre-booking available on www.knwrld.com. Morning screenings for large groups on Saturdays only.

H Chaplin's Friends: The Writers' Club

This film is based on the real story of a retired middle-aged reviewer who sets up a creative writing workshop: one of the women among his students is actually a well-known novelist that he has always disliked. Showtimes: 3:45 p.m. to 11.45 p.m

Part 3

Questions 11-15

For each question, choose the correct answer.

How to train your dog

15 year-old Pete Grayson tells us about his hobby, training dogs

Many families today also include a pet and there are lots of us who enjoy the quiet company of a cat or the relaxing presence of a goldfish. However, lots of people would rather have a dog as their four-legged friend.

Unfortunately, dogs aren't as easy to look after as you might expect when you finally get your first puppy. You have to feed them, walk them at least 3 times a day and play with them. Dogs also have to be trained to live with people, but there are some owners who don't understand this, which means that their dogs can develop annoying habits like barking all the time, jumping on people, or even biting strangers.

First of all, dogs need to be taught to be friendly to any human being. Most owners forget that dogs can't understand words as we do, so most communication should take place through body language or what you do. Dogs won't stop being aggressive if you just talk to them or even punish them but you can successfully teach them to behave well if you remember to reward them whenever they do what you want them to do.

Finally, remember dogs are animals that used to living in groups ('packs'), so they hate being alone. Although they now live in homes they still need to be part of a family. It's important to make time to go for walks and play with them, or they will never see you as the pack leader they can trust. If you behave like the boss of the pack, your dog will do anything to make you happy and proud.

Paper 1 Reading — Test 4

11 Pete says that people

- **A** often prefer owning a dog.
- **B** hardly ever have a pet.
- **C** are mostly interested in cats and goldfish.
- **D** don't usually have dogs because they're noisy.

12 Pete thinks that dogs

- **A** can be annoying if you don't feed them and play with them.
- **B** bark and bite people if they don't often go out.
- **C** are harder to take care of than people think.
- **D** are easy to look after because they're friendly.

13 How can people successfully communicate with their dog?

- **A** By telling them what to do in a loud voice.
- **B** By punishing them when they don't do what you want.
- **C** By using signals and showing them with hands.
- **D** By speaking more slowly than with a person.

14 Dogs are trained more easily if

- **A** you use a soft voice to talk to them.
- **B** you give them something nice when they do the right thing.
- **C** you show them that you are stronger than they are.
- **D** they are never punished for aggressive behaviour.

15 Which sentence best sums up the last paragraph?

- **A** You must treat your dog as a human being if you want it to respect people.
- **B** You must act as your family group leader if you want your dog to respect you.
- **C** Dogs are more fun to live with than any other pet because they are cleverer.
- **D** Dogs become aggressive when they spend too much time on their own.

Part 4

Questions 16-20

Five sentences have been removed from the text below.
For each space, choose the correct answer.
There are three extra sentences which you do not need to use.

Maths in the kitchen
by Sara Addari

I've been a Maths teacher for 20 years and I still enjoy doing my job. Teaching reminds you that you keep learning even when you are on the other side of the classroom. **16** This is why it came as no surprise when I felt it was time for something new: I decided to go back to school and train to be a cook.

This wasn't the first change I'd made in my life: I had studied Engineering at university and had gone to work for a software company. However, I left my job after three years to start teaching Maths and Physics at high school. **17** For five years I was often worried about a test I had to take, or frustrated because one of my teachers had treated me unfairly. Of course, I also had to deal with a heavier workload because I had less time to prepare lesson plans, attend meetings and mark my students' tests. **18**

I suppose being a student again made me a better teacher: we tend to forget what it means to get ready for an exam and we think teenagers shouldn't complain about homework or strict teachers. **19**
When I finally passed my exam at the vocational cooking school I was thrilled and proud. **20** That's why I'm going to take a break for a year from my teaching job and go on to apply for a professional pastry and baking school. Next year I'll forget about numbers and only focus on learning how to make delicious cakes and beautiful desserts. I've always been fond of cooking, especially cakes and desserts in general, so this will be a dream come true.

Paper 1 Reading — Test 4

A It felt like opening the door to a whole new world of opportunities.

B I started to feel bored with teaching so I stopped working at school.

C Despite this experience, joining a 5-year evening course while teaching morning classes wasn't exactly a piece of cake.

D I'd like to work in a restaurant as a pastry chef in the future.

E Studying can be very stressful.

F My students gave me a lot of support during the final exam.

G It also keeps you young at heart.

H It was so hard that I sometimes wondered if I had made the right choice.

Test 4 Paper 1 Reading

Part 5

Questions 21-26

For each question, choose the correct answer.

How can you improve your memory?

Whether it's new technology, a foreign language, or an advanced skill, scientists have proved there are four (21) _____ you can improve your memory and learn something faster.

First of all, if you imagine you are teaching someone (22) _____ the subject you are studying, you can speed up your learning and remember more. Experts also suggest that short, frequent learning sessions are (23) _____ better than longer ones: anything less than 30 minutes is just not enough, but you shouldn't study new material for more than an hour (24) _____ the information is too much for the brain to take in.

Another important discovery is that (25) _____ it's faster to take notes on a laptop, using a pen and paper will help you learn better. When students write down what they listen to they can identify important ideas more quickly.

Finally, a team of researchers have (26) _____ out that getting some sleep in between study sessions can greatly improve your memory and reduce the time you spend revising.

21	A systems	B paths	C ways	D modes
22	A else	B other	C on	D what
23	A more	B much	C many	D most
24	A when	B because	C if	D as long as
25	A however	B despite	C unless	D although
26	A kept	B got	C worked	D found

Paper 1 Reading — Test 4

Part 6

Questions 27-32

For each question, write the correct answer.
Write **one** word for each gap.

Book it!

It's called 'Book & Bed' and if you are fond of reading you might love spending a night there; however, **(27)** _____ you want to try it you must fly as far as Japan since it is in Tokyo.

Just like traditional bed and breakfast, this unique book temple offers cheap accommodation, but **(28)** _____ of checking into traditional rooms, the guests sleep in beds along rows of shelves. There are nearly two thousand books in a wide range of languages, including English and Japanese, of **(29)** _____ .

The 'Book & Bed' hotel is also very convenient as you **(30)** _____ have to cross the road to find restaurants of all kinds. Before turning into a very unusual guesthouse, 'Book & Bed' **(31)** _____ to be an *ryokan*, which is a traditional Japanese-style hotel.

Although the 'Book & Bed' hotel can't compete with 5-star hotels, it is the right choice for tourists that enjoy being in a unusual, interesting place **(32)** _____ they can have a good time and relax.

Test 4 Paper 2 Writing

Part 1

You **must** answer this question.
Write your answers in about **100 words** on the answer sheet.

Question 1

Read this email from your e-pal Aidan and the notes you have made.

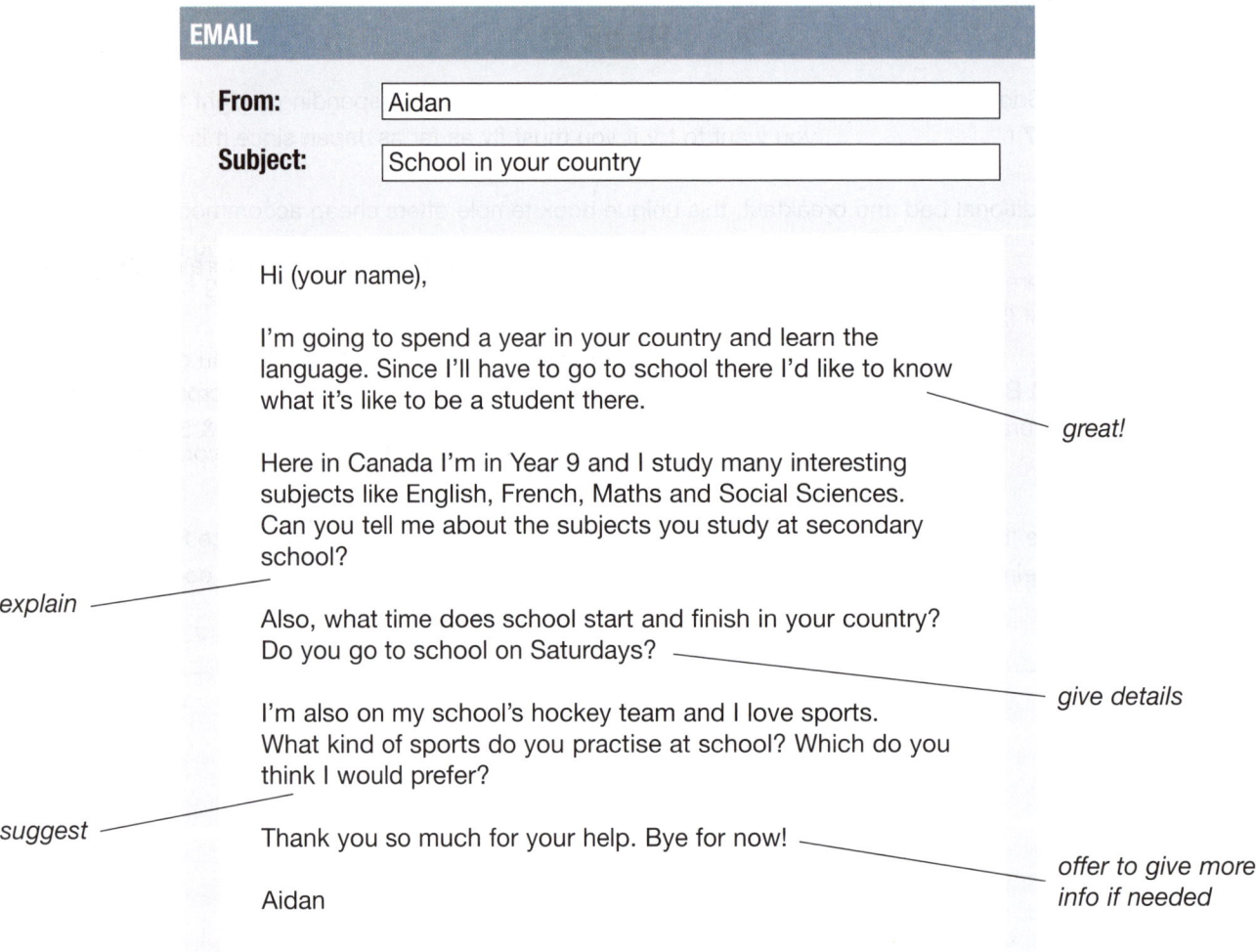

Write your **email** to your friend Aidan using **all the notes**.

Part 2

Choose **one** of these questions.
Write your answer in about **100 words** on the answer sheet.

Question 2

You see this notice in a bookshop.

THE JOYS OF READING

What sort of books do you enjoy reading?
Can reading help you to improve your life?
Why / Why not?
Write an article answering these questions and we will publish the best one in the bookshop's weekly magazine.

Write your **article**.

Question 3

You must write a story for your English teacher.
Your story must begin with this sentence.

> Mary picked up the bottle from the sand and saw there was a message in it.

Write your **story**.

Test 4 Paper 3 Listening

Part 1

 Questions 1-7

For each question, choose the correct answer.

1 What is the girl going to have for dinner?

A □   B □   C □

2 Which souvenir does the boy decide to buy?

A □   B □   C □

3 Where is Dave calling from?

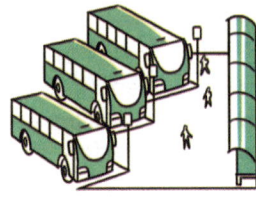      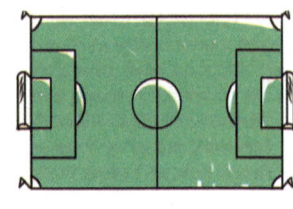

A □   B □   C □

Paper 3 Listening — Test 4

4 Which building is the museum?

A ☐   B ☐   C ☐

5 How much did the boy pay for the computer game?

      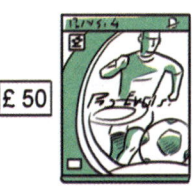

A ☐   B ☐   C ☐

6 What did Carol's mother use to do?

A ☐   B ☐   C ☐

7 Which pet would the girl like to get?

A ☐   B ☐   C ☐

Test 4 — Paper 3 Listening

Part 2

 Questions 8-13

For each question, choose the correct answer.

8   You will hear two teenagers talking about a new librarian. What do they think about her?
   - A   She isn't as well organised as the old librarian.
   - B   She is too young to work properly.
   - C   It won't take long before she learns how to do the job.

9   You will hear a boy and a girl talking about a smartphone. What does the boy complain about?
   - A   He can't download songs.
   - B   He can't turn up the volume.
   - C   The headphone's jack isn't working.

10 You will hear a girl talking to a friend on the phone. What is she going to do first?
   - A   going to the dentist
   - B   meeting her friend Sally
   - C   going to basketball practice

11 You will hear a boy and a girl talking. Why didn't the girl buy the shampoo?
   - A   She had to spend too much on Mark's video game.
   - B   She used the money to get Lewis a present.
   - C   She didn't need it.

12 You will hear a boy talking to his teacher on a school trip. Where are they?
   - A   at an old stadium
   - B   at a theatre
   - C   at a cinema

13 You will hear an athlete talking about her sport. What does she say about it?
   - A   You have to follow a special diet.
   - B   You don't need to work too hard.
   - C   You have no time for other activities.

Paper 3 Listening — Test 4

Part 3

🎧 **Questions 14-19**

For each question, write the correct answer in the gap.
Write **one** or **two words** or a **number** or a **date** or a **time**.

You will hear a man talking about a short story contest.

The Stratford Short Fiction Competition

Send in by: **(14)** _____
maximum word count for the Short Fiction Competition: 2,200 with no **(15)** _____
maximum word count for the Flash Fiction Competition: **(16)** _____

Last year's winner: 'Mind if I join you?' by Agnes Jepsen from **(17)** _____
Buy collections from this year and past years at www.**(18)** _____.com or from major online stores.

For those buying on our website this year's collections will be **(19)** 30_____ off.

Test 4 Paper 3 Listening

Part 4

 Questions 20-25

For each question, choose the correct answer.

You will hear an interview with a Mandarin teacher talking about his job.

20 How did he start teaching Mandarin?
   A   He saw a notice in a Chinese restaurant.
   B   He began teaching it at university.
   C   His girlfriend introduced him to a language school's manager.

21 According to Lenny, the most difficult thing to teach is
   A   pronunciation.
   B   grammar.
   C   vocabulary.

22 What does Lenny do during the first ten lessons?
   A   He teaches his students about the five different stresses.
   B   He gives them a lot of homework.
   C   He focuses on as much vocabulary as possible.

23 Lenny says he
   A   doesn't usually teach his students how to write characters.
   B   teaches his students how to recognise characters more easily.
   C   asks his students to learn at least 100 most common words.

24 What does Lenny advice Mandarin students to do?
   A   learn at least 5 words a day
   B   watch Chinese films or series with English subtitles
   C   read the news on Chinese newspapers

25 Next year Lenny plans to
   A   open his own foreign languages school.
   B   write a book for Mandarin learners.
   C   graduate from university.

Paper 1 Reading — Test 6

Part 6

Questions 27-32

For each question, write the correct answer.
Write **one** word for each gap.

Working as a clown
by Richard Kerr

I started my career as a clown when I was in my twenties. I **(27)** _____ to work as a magician before a colleague of mine introduced me to his best friend, who was a circus clown and needed a partner for his shows. That's **(28)** _____ my career started.

I spent 10 years working in several circuses. Although I had an agent at the time, I wanted to work **(29)** _____ my own, so I decided to try and get a job with the Starry Sky Circus. When I met the circus owner, he advised me to spend a term at the Clown School since he **(30)** _____ wanted professional performers. After 6 months' training, I joined the Starry Sky Circus and worked on the road for 5 years.

When others ask me how to become a great clown, I always tell **(31)** _____ that it depends on how much you enjoy the work: you won't be successful **(32)** _____ you really love what you do and commit to it.

Test 6 Paper 2 Writing

Part 1

You **must** answer this question.
Write your answers in about **100 words** on the answer sheet.

Question 1

Read this email from aunt Daphne and the notes you have made.

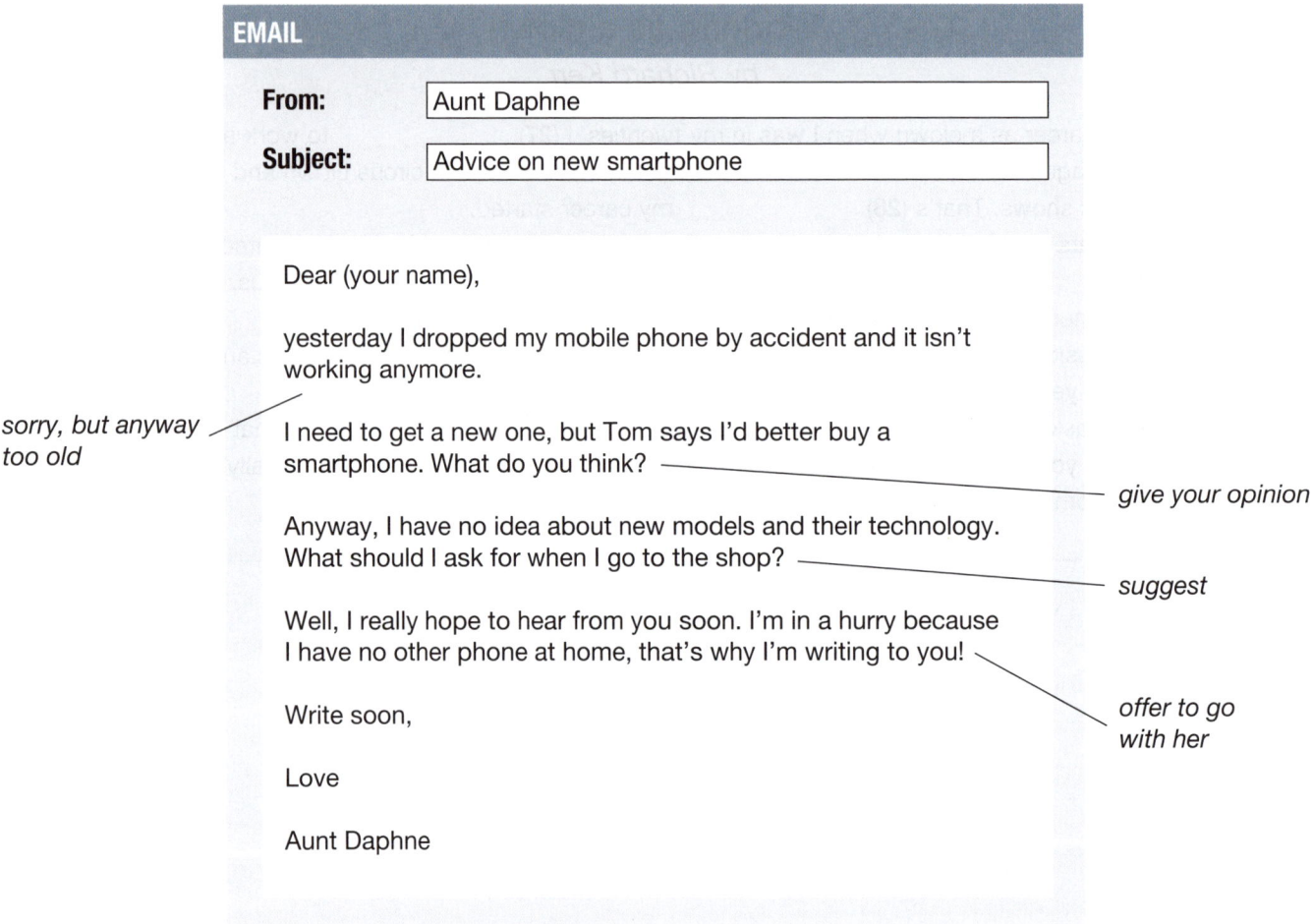

Write your **email** to your aunt Daphne using **all the notes**.

Paper 2 Writing — Test 6

Part 2

Choose **one** of these questions.
Write your answer in about **100 words** on the answer sheet.

Question 2

You see this ad on a wildlife magazine.

ARE YOU GREEN?

Do you think people should recycle more?
Why? / Why not?
What do you do to help the environment?

Write an article answering these questions.
The best article will win £100 prize
and be published on the school's One
Earth website next month.

Write your **article**.

Question 3

You must write a story for your English teacher.
Your story must begin with this sentence.

> It was a beautiful summer afternoon and the sun was shining when we set off.

Write your **story**.

Test 6 Paper 3 Listening

Part 1

 Questions 1-7

For each question, choose the correct answer.

1 Where were the girls supposed to meet?

A ☐

B ☐

C ☐

2 What time will the train leave?

A ☐

B ☐

C ☐

3 Which dress does the girl want to wear?

A ☐

B ☐

C ☐

Paper 3 Listening — **Test 6**

4 Which sport does the girl want to take up?

 A ☐

 B ☐

 C ☐

5 Where is the boy going first after school?

 A ☐

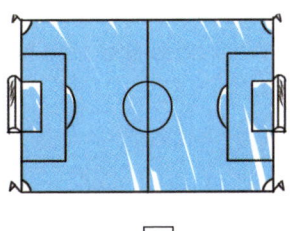 B ☐

 C ☐

6 What will Emma do this Sunday?

 A ☐

 B ☐

 C ☐

7 What does the boy decide to buy for his niece?

 A ☐

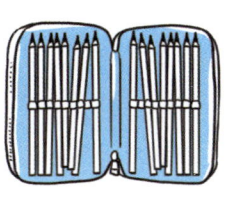 B ☐

 C ☐

Test 6 Paper 3 Listening

Part 2

 Questions 8-13

For each question, choose the correct answer.

8   You will hear a boy talking about a change in his life. What's he worried about?
    A   moving to a different town
    B   taking a French test
    C   going to a different school

9   You will hear two friends talking about what to watch on TV. What does the girl think about the zombie film?
    A   It's boring.
    B   It's frightening.
    C   It's thrilling.

10 You will hear a woman talking to her son. What does she want him to do now?
    A   tidy his room
    B   cut the grass in the garden
    C   do the shopping

11 You will hear two teenagers who have just been ice-skating. How does the girl feel about it?
    A   She didn't enjoy it very much because it was too cold.
    B   She enjoyed it but thinks it was too expensive.
    C   She's glad they didn't have to queue up to skate.

12 You will hear two people talking. How did the boy feel after the show?
    A   worried
    B   annoyed
    C   relieved

13 You will hear a boy and a girl talking about volleyball. Why did the boy stop playing?
    A   He didn't enjoy it any more.
    B   He didn't like the coach.
    C   He wanted to have enough time to go cycling.

Paper 3 Listening — Test 6

Part 3

 Questions 14-19

For each question, write the correct answer in the gap.
Write **one** or **two words** or a **number** or a **date** or a **time**.

You will hear a teacher talking to his students on a trip.

School trip to Stratford

Arriving in Stratford at (14) _____

Morning activities

- 10.00 a.m. - 11.00 a.m.: Anne Hathaway's (15) _____ - 500 years old

- 11.15 a.m. - midday: the Butterfly Farm — collection of insects and spiders and see the (16) _____

Lunch

- 1 o'clock - 2.30 p.m.: picnic in the (17) _____ near the river Avon

Afternoon activities

- 2.45 p.m.: visit Shakespeare's birthplace trust

- 4.15 p.m.: shopping for (18) _____

Teacher's phone number: (19) _____

Test 6 — Paper 3 Listening

Part 4

 Questions 20-25

For each question, choose the correct answer.

You will hear an interview with Amrita Bakshi talking about her life.

20 Amrita remembers she first took interest in computers when
   A she thought she wanted to be like her father.
   B she started using a computer at school.
   C she helped her teacher to solve a problem.

21 The first thing Amrita created was
   A an app for learning English verbs.
   B a computer program that looked like an app.
   C a tablet that helped students to learn foreign languages.

22 How old was Amrita when she sold her first app?
   A seven
   B nine
   C eleven

23 What is possible thanks to 'deep learning'?
   A to understand road signs when you drive
   B to tell your TV to turn off
   C to have a computer as a teacher

24 What makes Amrita different from other teenagers?
   A She has no friends her age.
   B She doesn't go to school.
   C She doesn't need to take exams.

25 What has Amrita done so far?
   A She's developed a computer game.
   B She's created a program to prevent illnesses.
   C She's written her first book.

Paper 4 Speaking — Test 6

Part 1 (2-3 minutes)

Phase 1

The interlocutor asks the same questions to candidate A and candidate B.

Interlocutor Good morning.
Can I have your mark sheets, please?
I'm (*interlocutor's name*) and this is (*assessor's name*).

What's your name?
How old are you?

	Back-up Prompts
Where do you come from?	Do you live in *name of town/city/region*?
Are you a student?	Do you study?
What school do you go to?	What subject do you study?

Thank you.

Phase 2

The interlocutor asks some personal questions to each candidate.
Ask Candidate A first.

Back-up Prompts

Interlocutor **Candidate A**

	Back-up Prompts
Do you have any hobby? Tell us about it.	What do you do in your free time?
What's your favourite part of the day? Why?	Do you like mornings? Why/Why not?

Candidate B

Tell us about your favourite food.	What's your favourite food? Why?
Where do you live?	Where do you come from?

Thank you.

Test 6 Paper 4 Speaking

Part 2 (2-3 minutes)

The interlocutor gives each candidate a photograph with a different topic.

Interlocutor Now I'd like each of you to talk on your own about something. I'm going to give each of you a photograph and I'd like you to talk about it.
A, here is your photograph. It shows **people playing sports**.
B, you just listen.
A, please tell us what you can see in the photograph.

A

Back-up prompts
- Talk about the people/person.
- Talk about the place.
- Talk about other things in the photograph.

Interlocutor Thank you.

Interlocutor B, here is your photograph. It shows **father and son at home**.
A, you just listen.
B, please tell us what you can see in the photograph.

B

Back-up prompts
- Talk about the people/person.
- Talk about the place.
- Talk about other things in the photograph.

Interlocutor Thank you.

Paper 4 Speaking   Test 6

Part 3 (2-3 minutes)

Interlocutor Now, in this part of the test you're going to talk about something together for about two minutes. I'm going to describe a situation to you.

**You and your classmate are going to suggest an after-school activity to do after class once a week. Here are some ideas to choose from.
Talk together and say which activity would be the most interesting and fun for students.**

All right? Now, talk together.

Part 4 (3 minutes)

The interlocutor asks questions related to what candidates discussed in Part 3.

Interlocutor What do you enjoy doing in your free time?
Which after-class activities does your school organise?
Do you think after-school activities are useful for students? Why? / Why not?
Which hobbies would you like to take up in the future?
Do you play any musical instrument?

Thank you. That is the end of the test.

Select any of the following prompts, as appropriate:
- **How/What about you?**
- **Do you agree?**
- **What do you think?**

Test 7 Paper 1 Reading

Part 1

Questions 1-5

For each question, choose the correct answer.

1

EMAIL

To: 1st year students
From: Mrs Liao

This is to remind you that your essays are due on 31st May. After this date, students will not be allowed to take the final exam in June.

A   Students must write their essays between the end of May and the end of June.

B   Students can take the June exam as long as they send their essays to the teacher on time.

C   If students forget to give the teacher their essays they'll be able to take the exam in June.

2

Luke, I have a History test tomorrow so I need you to bring back the book I lent you as soon as possible. I'm at home until 5. Anna

A   Anna is going to pick up her book from Luke's home at 5.

B   Luke has to return the book he borrowed from Anna.

C   Anna wants Luke to lend her his History book this afternoon.

3

SCHOOL NOTICE
For security reasons parents are not allowed to park in the staff car park

A   It is dangerous for parents to be in this staff car park.

B   Staff cannot park cars for parents.

C   Parents must park their cars somewhere else.

Paper 1 Reading | **Test 7**

4
> **How to save a file: drag and drop into folder and wait until download is over to click it open**

A You must move a file into a folder to save it.

B To open a file, open the 'download' folder.

C Open the folder with a click to drag and drop the file.

5

> **Please do not feed the animals as it makes them ill. If you are caught doing so, you will be asked to leave.**

This sign

A explains to visitors how to feed the animals.

B warns visitors not to give the animals anything to eat.

C tells visitors they cannot stay in the zoo if they are eating.

Test 7 Paper 1 Reading

Part 2

Questions 6-10

For each question, choose the correct answer.

The young people below all want to go to a summer festival.
On the opposite page there are descriptions of eight different festivals.
Decide which festival would be the most suitable for the young people below.

6  Jo likes reading, especially about different countries and cultures. He's also good at cooking and would really like the opportunity to learn new ways to cook from an expert.

7  Sally has lots of different hobbies and really enjoys making things with her hands. She would love to go to lots of different festivals, but she can't spend too much money or travel too far.

8  Archie loves technology and science, and really enjoys watching films that are set in the future. He loves his dog, Buster, and would like to find a festival that allows pets.

9  Rosa is into theatre and modern dance music. She would like to be a DJ when she's older. She wants to understand the technology behind the music more.

10  Conrad enjoys good food but mainly eating it, not cooking it. He likes finding out about other cultures and traditions and is thinking about learning flamenco guitar.

FESTIVALS!

A Book Festival

We have over 100 stalls at our festival with books on everything! Science, music, animals and more! TV's celebrity chef, George Hamley, will also be reading from his new novel *Recipe for success* on Saturday afternoon. There are also special sessions on how to become a writer and the future of e-books.

B World Food Festival

Food lovers, this is your festival. Come and discover a variety of tastes and flavours from across the continents. Jenny Morell, author of this year's best-selling cake baking book, will be giving a master class – you'll need to reserve your place quickly for that. Signed copies of her book will be available to buy after the class.

C World Music Festival

A day of music from around the world. We'll have traditional folk music from different countries as well as some of the most popular DJs in the UK today. Lots of tasty food from around the world too in case you get hungry. This is a pet-friendly event as we want this to be a fun day for all the family!

D Science Festival

For all you young scientists, come and get your hands on the latest technology at this year's festival. There's a special focus on electronic music and the chance to try making your own music. If that's not enough, you can be sure to be amazed by our robot theatre performance.

E Theatre Festival

It's back again! Our famous international theatre festival. All our big theatres will be involved, as well as a number of other smaller venues. You can walk through the city centre and find some street performances for free, and even get involved – ideal if you've always wanted to be on stage!

F Pet Festival

You'll be amazed by some of the animals at our festival this year. We have the usual 'Strangest pet' competition and it's a good opportunity to bring your pet and get advice on training from the experts. Look out for our special guest, too, the famous robot dog, Woofer, from this summer's hit sci-fi movie *Dogs in Space*!

G Art Festival

Art galleries will open their doors and there will be free entry with a festival pass. Art classes, including sculpture, are available too. There's a special exhibition on people and animals at the Portrait Gallery, where you can see paintings of celebrities with their pets.

H Open Doors Festival

Local artists will open their homes for people to visit and see their works of art, from jewellery to dressmaking. A perfect way to meet your talented neighbours. You can buy something individual and local, or you can just look for free.

Paper 1 Reading

Part 3

Questions 11-15

For each question, choose the correct answer.

Watching the veggies grow
15-year-old Sean McFarrell talks about his hobby, gardening

If you ask people 'What do teenagers do in their free time?', most people would reply saying that teenagers just want to do sport, play video games or listen to music. It's not surprising, I suppose – after all, I do all of those things. I also spend quite a lot of time surfing the net and watching TV.

But I'm not your typical teenager. Ever since I was a child I've had another hobby – I really enjoy growing vegetables and plants. If I'm honest, I'd even say that gardening is worth more to me than the most expensive tablet or smartphone!

We don't have a huge garden to do this where I live with my family. However, my grandparents have a lovely vegetable garden behind their cottage. Now that they're a bit older it's my garden and that's where I enjoy spending my free time when I'm not at school or playing basketball.

Unfortunately, It's not always convenient as I have to travel 20 miles to get to my grandparents' home. That's quite a long time to spend travelling, especially when I'm busy with schoolwork. My parents think I should get a different hobby closer to our home. But there are several reasons I don't let anyone else look after my garden. My plants help me to relax and keep my stress under control. They are also a way for me to keep seeing my grandparents regularly.

Sometimes when you're at school, with lots of homework, tests and exams, it seems like there is almost no time left for your family and friends. Actually, you don't even have time for yourself. With my plants and vegetables, I can be myself.

There's a final great lesson that plants can teach you: patience. Nowadays we expect to get whatever we want immediately. The internet has made us lazy – we've forgotten what it means to work and wait for something to happen. A vegetable garden can teach you to allow some time before a plant grows, a flower opens and a fruit is sweet enough to pick and eat.

Paper 1 Reading — Test 7

11 In the first paragraph Sean says that

  A teenagers always have hobbies such as sport and music.
  B he doesn't like playing sport or listening to music.
  C he is different to most teenagers although he likes some of the same things.
  D gardening is more expensive than smartphones or tablets.

12 Sean's parents think

  A he should give up gardening as there isn't enough time.
  B he should do something else instead of gardening.
  C he should ask someone else to look after his grandparents' garden.
  D he is too busy at school to spend time on gardening.

13 Which of these advantages does Sean mention?

  A His plants remind him who he actually is.
  B Looking after his garden helps him with his schoolwork.
  C When Sean takes care of the garden his parents are less stressed.
  D Gardening allows him to stay in touch with his friends.

14 Gardening is an excellent way to

  A learn how long it takes for plants to produce fruit.
  B remember that it takes time to achieve what you want.
  C stop wasting your time on the Internet.
  D understand how to look after plants in a fast, efficient way.

15 Which of the following sentences sums up Sean's ideas?

  A People would feel less stressed out if they started looking after a garden.

  C The best thing about gardening is that it makes you do better at school.

  B You mustn't take up gardening if you dislike travelling very frequently.

  D Gardening can be satisfying unless you want quick results.

129

Part 4

Questions 16-20

Five sentences have been removed from the text below.
For each space, choose the correct answer.
There are three extra sentences which you do not need to use.

The origins of the Olympic Games
by Yulia Carmichael

The greatest show of sporting excellence in the world began thousands of years ago in Olympia as a part of a religious festival to the Greek god Zeus. The first Olympic Games were held in 776 BC. **16** Back then time was measured in four-year periods known as Olympiads.

The ancient Greeks believed that competition encouraged excellence. The Olympiads were not only celebrated with sporting events, though. **17** You can read about them all in classical works of literature like Homer's *Iliad* or Virgil's *Aeneid*.

For the first thirteen games the ancient Greek Olympic Games featured just one event known as the 200-yard dash, a race where athletes had to run as fast as they could. **18** The new competitions included boxing, donkey riding and even a foot race: the competitors had to wear heavy equipment. After some time the five different sports were given the name of *pentathlon*. There was also another competition called *pankration*, where two competitors had to fight each other in any way they liked. **19**

In 391 AD, however, the Roman emperor Theodosius stopped these ancient Greek practices, so the world had to say goodbye to the Olympic Games. **20** Today, the summer and winter Olympics bring thousands of world-class champions together from all around the world, uniting billions of fans for the world's most exciting sporting competition.

Paper 1 Reading — Test 7

A The first Olympic champion in 776 BC was a baker named Coroebus.

B It was in 1896 that the modern Olympic Games were held again in Athens, Greece.

C This year became the basis for the earliest Greek calendar.

D The only thing that wasn't allowed was biting.

E Then, over time new exciting contests were added.

F Music, singing and poetry contests were held as well.

G This feeling was shared by many of the athletes.

H The origin of the Olympics Games is surrounded by mystery and legend.

Paper 1 Reading

Part 5

Questions 21-26

For each question, choose the correct answer.

Owls

Owls are birds whose large family includes about 200 species; they are typically active at night so they can see very well. They have a broad head, and very large wings that **(21)** _____ them to fly silently.

All owls are birds of prey and live mainly **(22)** _____ a diet of meat: they hunt small mammals **(23)** _____ rabbits or mice, insects, and other birds, although a few types prefer hunting fish. Since owls can be found in nearly **(24)** _____ parts of the world and across many different ecosystems, different types of owl have different hunting habits.

Their eyesight is particularly good and it helps owls to catch smaller animals to eat. Owls can't move their eyes in any **(25)** _____ , so they turn their heads to view what is around them. **(26)** _____ moving their head in this way, they make hardly any noise and they can hunt more easily.

21	A allow	B do	C leave	D make
22	A with	B on	C for	D at
23	A such	B as	C like	D how
24	A all	B every	C each	D whole
25	A position	B side	C area	D direction
26	A By	B Since	C While	D For

Paper 1 Reading

Part 6

Questions 27-32

For each question, write the correct answer.
Write **one** word for each gap.

My first teacher
by Gwen Pauls

When I think of the people **(27)** _____ have had an important role in my life, I always think about my primary school teacher, whose name was Mary Stetson.

She started every class in the morning by asking us all what we'd done the day before and telling **(28)** _____ what had happened to her. Her life wasn't very exciting, **(29)** _____ we were all interested **(30)** _____ listening to her funny stories.

When I was older, I realised the reason why we all liked her classes so **(31)** _____ was because we were having fun and learning at the same time. I think this is why I **(32)** _____ found going to school boring.

Test 7 Paper 2 Writing

Part 1

You **must** answer this question.
Write your answers in about **100 words** on the answer sheet.

Question 1

Read this email from your friend Zac and the notes you have made.

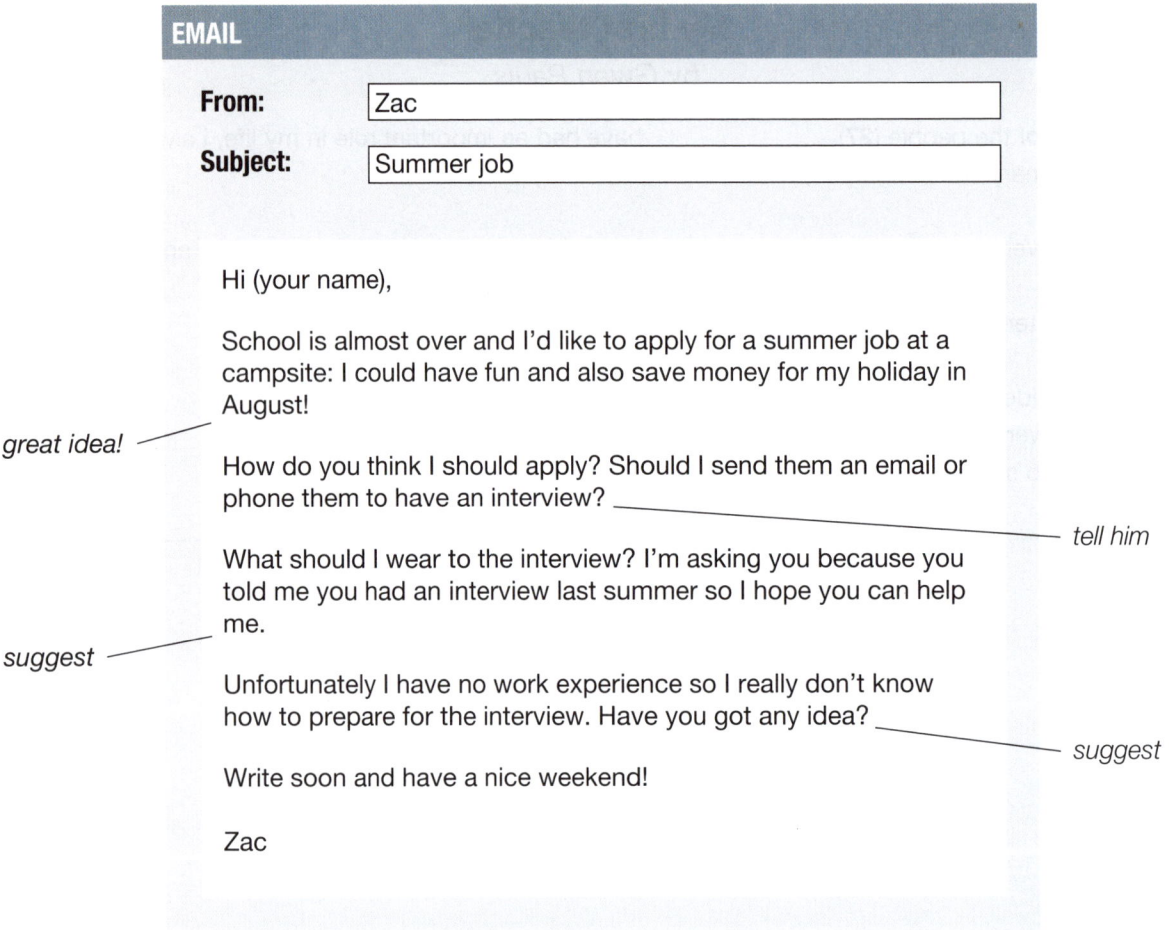

Write your **email** to your friend Zac using **all the notes**.

134

Paper 2 Writing — Test 7

Part 2

Choose **one** of these questions.
Write your answer in about **100 words** on the answer sheet.

Question 2

You see this ad on a website.

SOCIAL MEDIA
Do you often use social media?
Are social networks a good way to make friends?
Why / Why not?
Send us your article answering these questions
and we will post the best one on our website.

Write your **article**.

Question 3

You must write a story for your English teacher.
Your story must begin with this sentence.

> *I was reading in my bedroom when the light suddenly went out.*

Write your **story**.

Test 7 Paper 3 Listening

Part 1

 Questions 1-7

For each question, choose the correct answer.

1 What does Jane's grandfather look like?

A ☐

B ☐

C ☐

2 How much does the boy pay for his ticket?

A ☐

B ☐

C ☐

3 Which birthday present is Andrea wearing?

A ☐

B ☐

C ☐

4 How did the book end?

A ☐   B ☐   C ☐

5 When is the wedding anniversary?

A ☐   B ☐   C ☐

6 What should the girl do first?

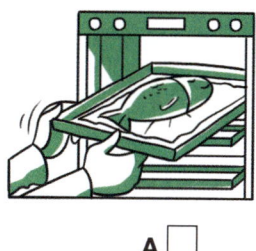 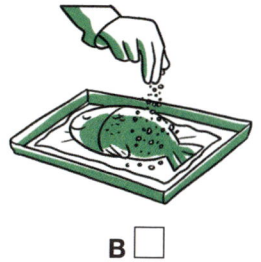 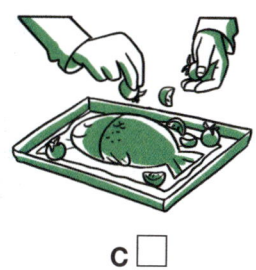

A ☐   B ☐   C ☐

7 Which film have they just seen?

A ☐   B ☐   C ☐

Test 7 Paper 3 Listening

Part 2

 Questions 8-13

For each question, choose the correct answer.

8 You will hear two classmates talking about a teacher: what do they disagree upon?
- **A** how she dresses
- **B** how she talks
- **C** how she explains things

9 You will hear two boys talking about camping. What didn't Vic like?
- **A** the weather
- **B** other people
- **C** the bed

10 You will hear a boy and a girl talking about a TV programme. What do they agree upon?
- **A** It's boring.
- **B** It's interesting.
- **C** It's terrible.

11 You will hear a mother and a daughter talking about a party. What does the girl complain about?
- **A** The food wasn't good.
- **B** The party was too crowded.
- **C** The cake wasn't sweet enough.

12 You will hear a dad and a daughter talking about a dog. How does the girl feel?
- **A** sad
- **B** happy
- **C** worried

13 You will hear a boy and a girl making plans for dinner. Which place do they choose to go to?
- **A** Pizza Hub
- **B** Sushi Bar
- **C** Hamburger Paradise

Paper 3 Listening — Test 7

Part 3

 Questions 14-19

For each question, write the correct answer in the gap.
Write **one** or **two words** or a **number** or a **date** or a **time**.

You will hear the museum's guide giving information to visitors.

The International Film Museum

Location:
- close to the International Film Festival

First Floor – Permanent Exhibition 'Film' (13 halls)

- over **(14)** _____ exhibits about the history of filmmaking
- objects on display: film scripts, **(15)** _____ and props
- information on special effects
- film director's hits including 'Metropolis' directed by Fritz Lang in **(16)** _____

Second floor – Marlene Dietrich Exhibition

- the actress' personal objects
- a section on **(17)** _____ and animated films

Ground floor

- bistro: tea and German cakes
- museum shop - **(18)** _____ ticket office

Visit our website at www.**(19)** _____.de

Test 7 — Paper 3 Listening

Part 4

 Questions 20-25

For each question, choose the correct answer.

You will hear an interview with inventor Luke Culotta talking about his job.

20 When did Luke take his first steps into inventing?
- **A** He made special slippers that a lot of people bought.
- **B** He realised he wanted to make things people needed.
- **C** He had always been a creative student at school.

21 What does Luke say about his first invention?
- **A** It wasn't anything new: he just changed a toy to make it more interesting.
- **B** It was a very original invention that children could play with in their rooms.
- **C** It wasn't popular until a company started selling it on TV.

22 Which of these objects did he most enjoy making?
- **A** a cushion with arms
- **B** a talking watch
- **C** a dog umbrella

23 Luke's company aims at
- **A** training European school students to become successful inventors.
- **B** helping both teenagers and adults to sell their inventions.
- **C** putting young inventors in contact with interested companies.

24 What is Luke's first suggestion for young inventors?
- **A** Apply for a patent to protect your idea from anyone trying to steal it.
- **B** Remember that patent rules are not the same everywhere.
- **C** Find a way to show your idea to companies that may like it.

25 What does Luke think about the Internet?
- **A** It helps people to increase their knowledge.
- **B** It makes people waste a lot of time and feel stressed out.
- **C** It controls people's lives, but it also helps them find new friends.

Paper 4 Speaking — Test 7

Part 1 (2-3 minutes)

Phase 1

The interlocutor asks the same questions to candidate A and candidate B.

Interlocutor   Good afternoon.
Can I have your mark sheets, please?
I'm (*interlocutor's name*) and this is (*assessor's name*).

What's your name?
How old are you?

Back-up Prompts

Where do you come from?   Do you live in *name of town/city/region*?
Are you a student?   Do you study?
What do you study?   What subject do you study?

Thank you.

Phase 2

The interlocutor asks some personal questions to each candidate.
Ask Candidate A first.

Back-up Prompts

Interlocutor   **Candidate A**

Tell us about your classmates.   Tell us about the people in your class.
Do you like travelling? Why?   Where would you like to go on your next travel? Why?

Candidate B

Do you have any pet? What's it like?   Tell us about your pet. What's it like?
What did you do last summer?   Did you do anything last summer? What?

Thank you.

Test 7 — Paper 4 Speaking

Part 2 (2-3 minutes)

The interlocutor gives each candidate a photograph with a different topic.

Interlocutor Now I'd like each of you to talk on your own about something. I'm going to give each of you a photograph and I'd like you to talk about it.
A, here is your photograph. It shows **people in a kitchen**.
B, you just listen.
A, please tell us what you can see in the photograph.

A

Back-up prompts
- Talk about the people/person.
- Talk about the place.
- Talk about other things in the photograph.

Interlocutor Thank you.

Interlocutor B, here is your photograph. It shows **people in the mountains**.
A, you just listen.
B, please tell us what you can see in the photograph.

B

Back-up prompts
- Talk about the people/person.
- Talk about the place.
- Talk about other things in the photograph.

Interlocutor Thank you.

Paper 4 Speaking — Test 7

Part 3 (2-3 minutes)

Interlocutor Now, in this part of the test you're going to talk about something together for about two minutes. I'm going to describe a situation to you.

Your grandparents are going to celebrate their 50th wedding anniversary. Suggest them different places they can go to. Talk together about the different holidays they could enjoy, and say which would be most suitable for them.

All right? Now, talk together.

Part 4 (3 minutes)

The interlocutor asks questions related to what candidates discussed in Part 3.

Interlocutor What kind of holiday do you prefer?
What's the most exciting holiday you have had?
Where are you going on holiday this year?
Would you like to go on a tour around the world?
Why / Why not?
Do you prefer the seaside or the mountains?

Thank you. That is the end of the test.

Select any of the following prompts, as appropriate:

- **How/What about you?**
- **Do you agree?**
- **What do you think?**

Test 8 — Paper 1 Reading

Part 1

Questions 1-5

For each question, choose the correct answer.

1

MAXIMUM WEIGHT NO MORE THAN TWENTY KILOS

A Checked baggage can be more than 20kg.

B There is a weight limit of 20kg.

C It's better if the object weighs 20kg.

2

THIS TOY IS SUITABLE FOR CHILDREN OVER 36 MONTHS

A You can give this to children younger than three.

B It is better to give this to older children.

C Children will play with this toy for a long time.

3

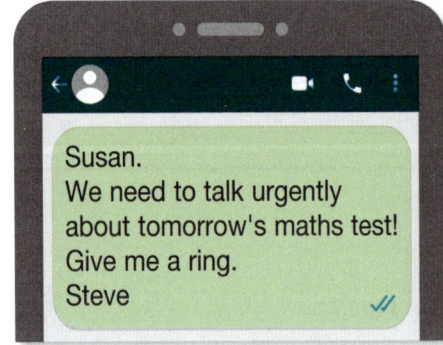

Susan.
We need to talk urgently about tomorrow's maths test! Give me a ring.
Steve

A Susan has to contact Steve soon.

B Steve expects to call Susan soon.

C Susan needs to talk to Steve tomorrow.

144

4

> **SCHOOL DANCE GROUP**
> Membership forms available from the school office until Friday

A   You must get your form before Friday.

B   You should get your form on Friday.

C   You won't be able to get your form after Friday.

5

> A smartphone was found in the library on Tuesday morning. To have it back, speak to Mr O'Donnell.

Ask Mr O'Donnell if...

A   you want to speak on the phone in the library.

B   you have lost a smartphone.

C   you have found a smartphone.

Test 8 Paper 1 Reading

Part 2

Questions 6-10

For each question, choose the correct answer.

The people below all want to join a sports class.
On the opposite page there are eight class descriptions.
Decide which class would be the most suitable for the people below.

6  Joanna already plays football at school, but she wants to be able to improve her skills. She'd like to play in competitions and possibly become a professional football player when she's older.

7  Ged likes being outside and meeting new people. He wants to join a club where he can have fun and try some different sports, but he doesn't want to take part in any competitions.

8  Gina wants to get fit. She can't swim and she's already quite busy with other clubs after school so she would like to find a club that has classes at different days and times.

9 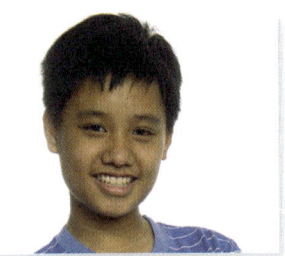 John likes team sports but he wants to try something different. He wants to be able to get fitter and stronger but also to relax. He needs something suitable for a complete beginner.

10  Zara loves being in the sea and she's a good swimmer, but she'd like to be more confident. She's eager to learn some new skills and possibly do some training for underwater swimming.

Sports centres

A High-kick

This is not your usual class! We use dance moves and weights in high-energy routines to help get you healthier. We offer a 10% discount if you book a course of ten Thursday classes at 6 p.m. or come along to our drop-in classes on Saturday mornings at 9.30 a.m. and just pay on the day.

B On the ball

We work with our local football team to provide training for young players who need to improve their technique. Club members have the chance to join the youth under-15s team and play in the regional league. Fridays 5 p.m.

C Aqua-fit

Forget the gym, jump in the pool! Get fit in the water whilst listening to some of the best tunes in pop music. Swimmers only, so we recommend that you join our beginners swimming course before joining this course if you can't swim yet. Wednesdays and Fridays at 5.30 p.m. in the main pool.

D On your marks!

We specialise in triathlon (running, cycling and swimming) and you'll be feeling healthier in no time. We focus on having a good time and we're also very sociable. We also have a five-a-side football team and a disco night once a month. Every Saturday 5-6.30 p.m.

E Kick off club!

For complete beginners and more experienced players, we offer football classes and matches for those who want to practise and play in a relaxed atmosphere. No competitions, no pressure, just fun and fitness! Beginners: Wednesdays at 5 p.m., and Improvers: Saturdays 10 a.m.

F Mind and body

A healthy mind is just as important as a healthy body and we use traditional yoga which will stretch your muscles and your brain. You'll be stronger but also calmer. If you're new to yoga that's no problem. Join us for a juice and a chat in the café after the class too! Saturdays at midday.

G On track

We are looking for experienced young athletes who are prepared to compete in our summer track and field games. We offer lots of athletic activities, including running, high jump and long jump. You can also choose to add swimming too. Tuesdays at 6.30 p.m.

H Making waves

Join our club to learn about special techniques for swimming outdoors. You'll start in the pool but then we put our new skills into practice outside. You can learn diving, and we offer a scuba diving option for an additional fee. Sundays 11 a.m.-1 p.m.

Part 3

Questions 11-15

For each question, choose the correct answer.

Going Greener!

Jodie, 15, talks about being an environmental youth volunteer

As a young child, I remember being fascinated by being outside. My mum used to take my sister and me to the woods near our house. She thought it was important we learned about the natural world. She would show us different trees and plants, and we would learn to recognise the different birds by their unique songs. I also remember that I got really upset whenever I saw litter. I couldn't believe what people had left behind – plastic bags, empty bottles. So many different animals and plants live in the forest – it's their home. I'm sure we would feel angry if someone left rubbish all over our homes! So, I used to take my rucksack and pick up the litter.

Now I'm older I've become a youth volunteer for a local environmental charity. That means I spend a few hours every weekend picking up rubbish, tidying public spaces and generally working for free. I'm not paid but I don't mind. To be honest, I enjoy it! The idea of sitting at home on the sofa watching another ridiculous programme on TV just makes me depressed.

Instead, if I think about the next park I'm going to clean up, I get quite excited. I like being active outside in the fresh air, and the end result is so satisfying: a clean and tidy green space for wildlife, as well as a safe, attractive place for other people to come and visit.

You may think I'm mad spending my weekends and days off like this. But think about it: what would it be like if we all did a little clearing up as a hobby? Our towns and countryside would be clean and pleasant, and a safe place for all of us to enjoy. I know I've got a rather unusual hobby, but it really helps me to feel calm and happy. It would be great if more people did something similar.

There are other advantages, too. I meet a lot of other young people who feel the same way as me about protecting the environment, so I have lots of new friends. One day I hope to use my experience to help me find a job working outside too.

Paper 1 Reading — Test 8

11 How did Jodie feel in the forest when she was a young child?

- **A** shocked that people visited the forest
- **B** angry that people took their rubbish home
- **C** sad that people made such a mess
- **D** ashamed that she picked up the litter

12 What does the writer feel about not being paid?

- **A** It's unfair.
- **B** It's depressing.
- **C** It's a waste of time.
- **D** It's not important.

13 The writer gets satisfaction from

- **A** doing activities outside.
- **B** working all the time.
- **C** seeing the difference her work makes.
- **D** meeting new people.

14 The writer says her hobby is

- **A** a bit crazy and strange.
- **B** more common than we may think.
- **C** a good way to relax.
- **D** safe for all the community.

15 Which statement best describes Jodie?

A Jodie is keen to keep the environment clean but wants to be paid.

C Jodie thinks people must keep the environment clean.

B Jodie prefers helping the environment than sitting at home.

D Jodie recommends making friends who think the same as you.

Part 4

Questions 16-20

Five sentences have been removed from the text below.
For each space, choose the correct answer.
There are three extra sentences which you do not need to use.

Body art

Do you think of yourself as a living work of art? Is there a picture or a name of someone that is so important to you that you would want it on your skin forever? It's clear that many people do. **16**

Although tattoos might seem to be a modern part of fashion, they have actually been with us for a very long time. **17** It seems that some of the first tattoos were a kind of treatment for illness. Archaeologists who research ancient Egypt have also discovered signs that images and symbols were painted on the skin. **18**

It's important to remember that a tattoo is supposed to be permanent. **19** However, even though it isn't easy, quite a lot of people change their mind and decide to get rid of their body tattoo. The most common reason for this is because they have a tattoo of someone's name.

Although tattoos are very common and generally accepted, you should still take your time before you get one. **20** When you are older and go for your interview for a job or a place at university, do you really want a tattoo to be showing? If not, choose a place on your body where it can be covered by clothes. For example, many women choose the ankle and for men the back of the shoulder is often a popular place.

Paper 1 Reading — Test 8

A They think they were put there to bring good luck.

B It's also important to think where on your body you want to have your tattoo.

C Other people wear jewellery instead.

D In the United States, for example, more than a quarter of adults have a tattoo.

E Tattoos were done differently in the past.

F The earliest evidence of tattoos is from around 5,000 years ago in central Europe.

G It's a good idea to check with your parents before getting a tattoo.

H It is possible to get your tattoo removed, but that will involve more pain and more money.

Test 8 Paper 1 Reading

Part 5

Questions 21-26

For each question, choose the correct answer.

Body language tricks

Everybody knows what it's like when you have to patiently wait to order food in a crowded café. There's a (21) _____ of unwritten rule based on the 'first come first served' principle, but research has recently found out that customers have other (22) _____ to get the waiter's attention.

After carefully watching how people behave in situations like these, a team of psychologists were able to identify the best body language to get served (23) _____ other people.

The most successful way seems to be standing in front of the person at the ordering desk and looking at him or her; (24) _____ people standing behind other customers typically have to wait longer than necessary. The researchers also point out that your chances of being served soon decrease if you talk to friends and read the menu while sitting down. (25) _____, waving your hand or nodding at the waiter isn't as effective as expected, whereas you will probably be served more quickly if you (26) _____ your wallet or cash in your hand.

21	A type	B deal	C sort	D lot
22	A ways	B modes	C behaviour	D signs
23	A after	B before	C with	D over
24	A while	B instead	C so	D as
25	A Suddenly	B Despite	C Of course	D Surprisingly
26	A carry	B keep	C take	D hold

Paper 1 Reading Test 8

Part 6

Questions 27-32

For each question, write the correct answer.
Write **one** word for each gap.

E-love for books

Last year, I got an e-book reader as a birthday gift.

At first I wasn't that enthusiast, even if I've always loved reading, (27) _____ I was a child; but no digital device would (28) _____ replace my paper books. It's not just about reading in itself, but it's a total experience: I really love the feel of the paper between my fingers and the smell of the pages as I read.
So, I thanked my aunt (29) _____ the gift, and I put it in the drawer of my table, where it remained for almost one year, until I decided (30) _____ give it a go. And then I discovered a whole new world. On an e-book reader you can store thousands of e-books: you can easily download and read (31) _____ within minutes, and they are also cheaper than paper books! It's amazing: you can carry your whole library in your bag!

Of course, e-books have small disadvantages, too. If your battery dies, you can't use your e-reader unless you recharge it – but you can easily find a solar power charger to carry with you.

An e-reader is more fragile than a paper book, so you should protect it (32) _____ water, or other damages, with a strong case.

Test 8 Paper 2 Writing

Part 1

You **must** answer this question.
Write your answers in about **100 words** on the answer sheet.

Question 1

Read this email from your English teacher, Miss Blair, and the notes you have made.

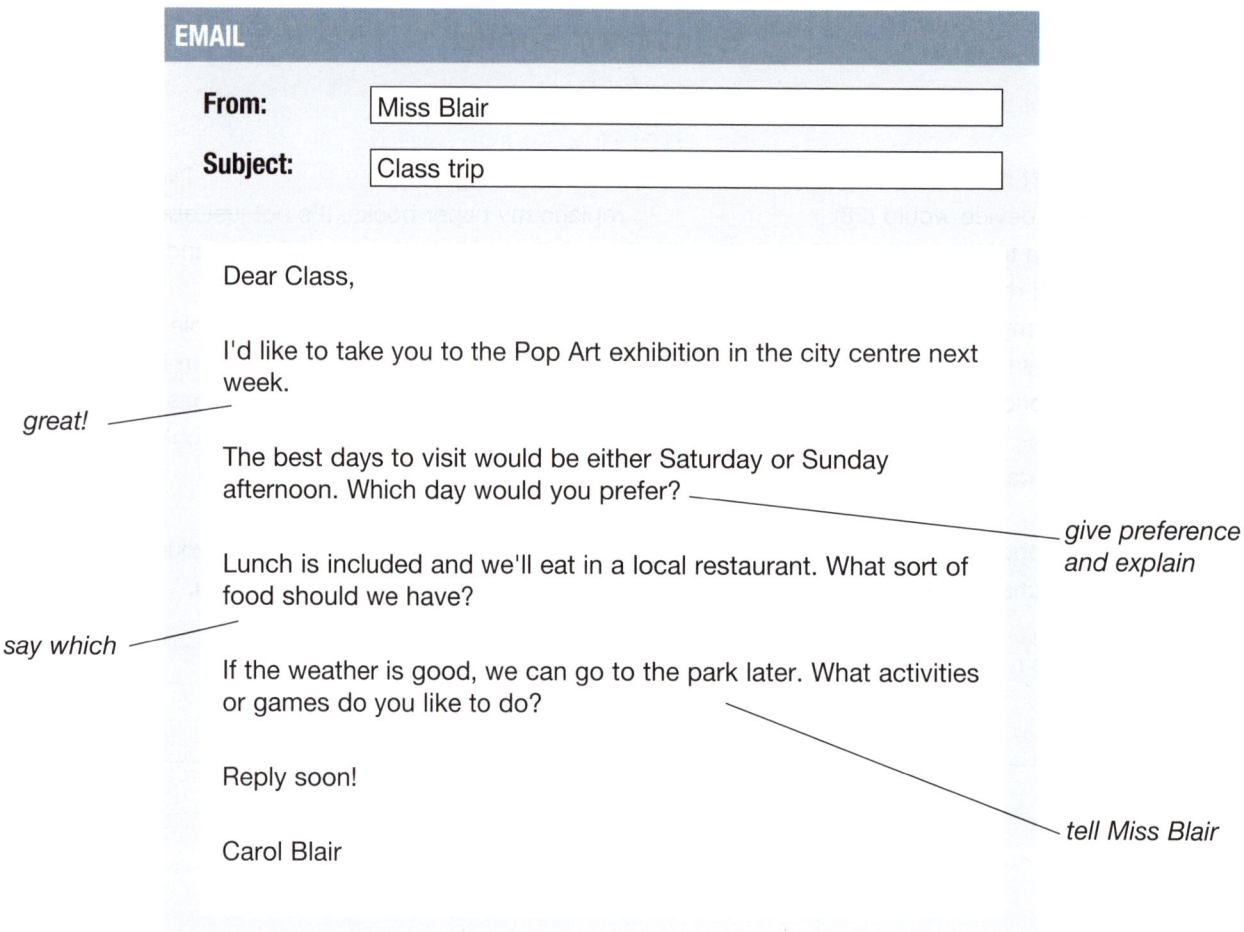

Write your **email** to Miss Blair using **all the notes**.

Paper 2 Writing — Test 8

Part 2

Choose **one** of these questions.
Write your answers in about **100 words** on the answer sheet.

Question 2

You see this announcement in a local newspaper.

NEWS

ARTICLES WANTED!
What was your best holiday?
Write an article telling us about
the best holiday you've ever had!
Where did you go? Who were you with?
Why did you enjoy it so much?
Your article may be published
in this school newsletter!

Write your **article**.

Question 3

Your English teacher has asked you to write a story.
Your story must begin with this sentence.

> Alex stood up, grabbed his phone and ran out of the room.

Write your **story**.

Test 8 Paper 3 Listening

Part 1

 Questions 1-7

For each question, choose the correct answer.

1 Where is the washing machine?

A ☐

B ☐

C ☐

2 Which team is she in?

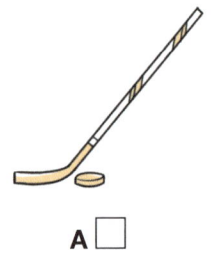

A ☐

B ☐

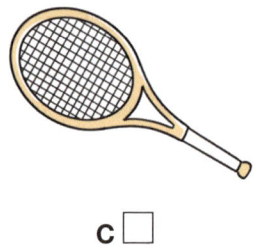

C ☐

3 Where are they going this weekend?

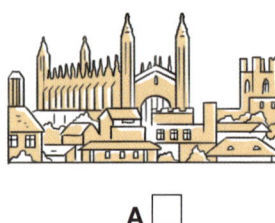

A ☐

B ☐

C ☐

Paper 3 Listening **Test 8**

4 What did she buy?

A ☐ B ☐ C ☐

5 How did they find out about the story?

A ☐ B ☐ C ☐

6 What should they move?

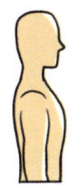 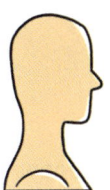 

A ☐ B ☐ C ☐

7 What is he going to do tomorrow?

A ☐ B ☐ C ☐

Test 8   Paper 3 Listening

Part 2

 Questions 8-13

For each question, choose the correct answer.

8   You will hear a boy talking about a school trip. How does he feel about the trip?
- **A** The museums were great.
- **B** There wasn't enough variety.
- **C** There was nothing to do in the city.

9   You will hear a girl telling a friend about the sports club she's just joined. How does the boy think she would feel like?
- **A** very happy
- **B** very busy
- **C** very tired

10   You will hear two friends talking about learning to play the violin. The girl advises the boy to
- **A** learn an easier instrument.
- **B** change the kind of music he plays.
- **C** make more of an effort.

11   You will hear two friends talking about a book. They agree that
- **A** it was too long.
- **B** the ending was good.
- **C** the characters were realistic.

12   You will hear two friends talking immediately after a concert. They don't agree about
- **A** the price.
- **B** the ability of the musicians.
- **C** the sound quality.

13   You will hear two friends discussing a new mobile phone. What is most important for the boy?
- **A** using the Internet
- **B** listening to music
- **C** taking photographs

Paper 3 Listening — Test 8

Part 3

 **Questions 14-19**

For each question, write the correct answer in the gap.
Write **one** or **two words** or a **number** or a **date** or a **time**.

You will hear a radio announcer explaining the details of a competition.

The 5th Annual Sound Radio Drawing and Painting Competition

The competition is open to all people aged 21 and (**14**) _____ .

There is a (**15**) _____ category for children younger than 10.

You must send an (**16**) _____ form to enter, and this must be signed by an adult if you're under 16.

The categories are: (**17**) _____ , watercolour and experimental.

Works must be sent by (**18**) _____ .

Prizes include 10 luxury (**19**) _____ painting sets for works of above-average quality.

Test 8 Paper 3 Listening

Part 4

 Questions 20-25

For each question, choose the correct answer.

You will hear an interview about global warming.

20 Global warming refers to
   A changes in seasonal temperature.
   B an increase in average global temperature.
   C wind and humidity for a given area.

21 The increase of average global temperatures has accelerated
   A over the past few decades.
   B over the past few years.
   C after the industrial revolution.

22 The countries which contribute the most to global warming are
   A the richest.
   B the most populated.
   C the poorest.

23 The United States emits
   A 42% of the world's total carbon.
   B 24% of the world's total carbon.
   C 12% of the world's total carbon.

24 China emits
   A 20% of the world's total carbon.
   B 21% of the world's total carbon.
   C 12% of the world's total carbon.

25 To pollute less and conserve energy
   A is useless to avoid climate change.
   B is only a duty of the governments.
   C is a way to contribute to reduce climate change.

Paper 4 Speaking — Test 8

Part 1 (2-3 minutes)

Phase 1

The interlocutor asks the same questions to candidate A and candidate B.

Interlocutor Good morning.
Can I have your mark sheets, please?
I'm (*interlocutor's name*) and this is (*assessor's name*).

What's your name?
How old are you?

	Back-up Prompts
Where do you come from?	Do you live in *name of town/city/region*?
Are you a student?	Do you study?
What do you study?	What subject do you study?

Thank you.

Phase 2

The interlocutor asks some personal questions to each candidate.
Ask Candidate A first.

Back-up Prompts

Interlocutor **Candidate A**

What did you do last yesterday afternoon?	Did you do anything yesterday afternoon? What?
Do you like watching TV? Why/Why not?	What's your favourite TV program? Why?

Candidate B

Do you like Mondays? Why/Why not?	What's your favourite day of the week? Why?
Tell us about your best friend.	Do you have a best friend? What's he/she like?

Thank you.

Test 8 Paper 4 Speaking

Part 2 (2-3 minutes)

The interlocutor gives each candidate a photograph with a different topic.

Interlocutor Now I'd like each of you to talk on your own about something. I'm going to give each of you a photograph and I'd like you to talk about it.
A, here is your photograph. It shows **a big city**.
B, you just listen.
A, please tell us what you can see in the photograph.

A

Back-up prompts
- Talk about the people/person.
- Talk about the place.
- Talk about other things in the photograph.

Interlocutor Thank you.

Interlocutor B, here is your photograph. It shows **people eating together**.
A, you just listen.
B, please tell us what you can see in the photograph.

B

Back-up prompts
- Talk about the people/person.
- Talk about the place.
- Talk about other things in the photograph.

Interlocutor Thank you.

Paper 4 Speaking — Test 8

Part 3 (2-3 minutes)

Interlocutor Now, in this part of the test you're going to talk about something together for about two minutes. I'm going to describe a situation to you.

**It's Saturday afternoon and two brothers don't know what to do. Talk together about the different things they could do, and decide which would be best for them.
Here is a picture with some ideas to help you.**

All right? Now, talk together.

Part 4 (3 minutes)

The interlocutor asks questions related to what candidates discussed in Part 3.

Interlocutor What kind of free-time activities are there where you live?
Which are best for young people? Why?
What activities do you like doing best? Why?
Are there any free-time activities that you would like to try?
What are they?

Thank you. That is the end of the test.

Select any of the following prompts, as appropriate:
- How/What about you?
- Do you agree?
- What do you think?

Test 1

Part 1 p. 16

Rubric 1: What did Jack do yesterday afternoon?
Elise Hi, Jack. How was the exhibition yesterday?
Jack Actually, I didn't go… I woke up with an awful toothache, so I called my dad and asked him if he could pick me up from home and take me to the dentist. It took ages to get there as there was a huge traffic jam. And when we got there, there was no parking space so Dad had to wait in the car for two hours while I was in hospital! At least, I'm feeling better now, so we can go to the exhibition together. What about this weekend?
Elise Poor you! OK, the weekend is perfect to go around a bit – see you!

Rubric 2: Why was the train cancelled?
Claire Sorry I'm late, Mum.
Mum What happened, Claire? I was a bit worried…
Claire The train was cancelled.
Mum Oh, there must be a strike then.
Claire Actually, everybody thought it was because of the rain, but then I heard an announcement that there was something blocking the railway line just outside the station. Anyway, it definitely takes longer by bus.

Rubric 3: What time does the German lesson usually start on Thursdays?
Man Good morning. Before starting class today I need to tell you there's a little change in our timetable next week.
Boy Is there any problem, Mr Kurtz?
Man No, not really. Instead of beginning at three forty, next Thursday we'll have our lesson at half past four. The Tuesday lesson will be at the usual time, twenty to three.
Girl Thanks Mr Kurtz.

Rubric 4: Where are Sarah and her family having their holiday this summer?
Thom Hi, Sarah. Have your parents booked your flight?
Sarah Yes, I can't wait to go! I've never been to South Africa before… we've decided to set off in February, though, because it's summer there.
Thom Oh, I thought you were going during the school holidays.
Sarah I talked to the teachers about it and they all said it wouldn't be a problem for just one week. Anyway, when school finishes I'll go to the mountains as usual. My parents can't stand crowded beaches or hot weather in summer…

Rubric 5: Where are Mum's keys?
Mum Have you seen my keys anywhere?
Peter Have you looked in your bag, Mum? you always keep them there.
Mum Yes, of course I have… and they aren't there!
Peter When did you last use them? Sometimes when you get back from the shops you put them on the shelf beside the door.
Mum Oh, you're right. There they are: I left them there when I got back with that heavy shopping bag.

Rubric 6: Who is Aidan's History teacher?
Aidan Who's the blonde woman over there? Is she your new History teacher?
Grainne No, actually my History teacher is a man, you know, the one with a moustache.
Aidan Oh, I know who that is! The bald man! He is quite old, is he?
Grainne That's the Art teacher! The History teacher has curly hair and looks much younger than that, anyway!

Rubric 7: Which photo does Cindy prefer?
Eddie Cindy I need your help! I want to put a photo of our school trip on my blog, but I can't make up my mind between the one we took in front of the church or this one, with you and me at the lake.
Cindy I like both of them, but I think this one is more interesting: the trees around us are magnificent! It's a pity you didn't take any picture of the view from the tower: it was amazing! That was my favourite part of the school trip!
Eddie Yeah, that's too bad…

Part 2 p. 18

Question 8
Girl So when do you usually help your parents with the housework?
Boy Mostly at weekends, because I have to go to school on the other days.
Girl And what do you do first?
Boy I usually start tidying my bedroom and my sister's room: she's too young, I don't mind helping her; I also have to clean the windows once a month: I can't stand doing it because it always rains afterwards.
Girl What about doing the washing up? I hate doing that!
Boy Do you? I don't. It's something I actually enjoy doing because I can listen to music and sing to myself in the kitchen while nobody's listening!

Question 9
Boy That was a great concert, wasn't it?
Girl I think it was OK. The guy on the guitar was a bit disappointing, wasn't he?
Boy No way. The music was perfect! And certainly not what I expected from this new band. The only thing I was annoyed about is that it was too loud, as usual. I mean, I couldn't even understand the words…
Girl Well, I guess I've never been to a pop music concert where the sound was too low. I wonder why they never check the sound walking around the room when it's crowded with screaming fans… It's a pity as the singer was quite good, though I could hardly hear her voice.
Boy Yeah, though I liked the way she sang.

Question 10
Girl 1 Have you tried the Zumba course? The instructor is so much fun and high energy. I've done three classes since we joined last week and I can't wait for the fourth this afternoon.
Girl 2 I don't know, I've never tried Zumba before… I prefer training with weights.
Girl 1 But we still have two weeks to try all the courses for free: remember they told us we can do all the courses on offer for three weeks. if I were you I'd try all of them. You can use the weight room when you want, anyway.
Girl 2 Yeah, you're right. Ok, I'll try it out today then. I hope it doesn't matter if I missed the first week…

Question 11
Girl Dad, can you pick me up from school this afternoon? I forgot I need to be home by five thirty before my piano lesson starts.
Dad Mmm, why didn't you tell me yesterday, Tanya? I have a few appointments at work so I need to cancel them.
Girl Sorry, Dad. I asked Mum too, but she's going to the dentist at a quarter to four so she wouldn't have enough time to get to school at half past four.
Dad Ok, don't worry. I'll be there when you leave school then. And please, don't be late! I need to get back to work by five.

Question 12
Lucy I'm not sure I've ever seen this one, when I first came to Paris with my parents last year.
Carl It doesn't surprise me: there are 37 bridges across the river Seine! The French teacher said it was built in nineteen hundred and it's listed as a historic monument.
Lucy It reminds me of the one we went over near Notre Dame Cathedral. It looks exactly the same, don't you think so?
Carl Yeah, but it's much smaller.
Lucy Let's ask the teachers if we can go across it and take picture: i think we can see the Eiffel Tower from there.

Question 13
Ms Crane Is everything clear, guys?
Boy Excuse me, Ms Crane, what's the word count?
Ms Crane You can use about two hundred words in 4 or 5 paragraphs, including the conclusion. And don't forget to introduce the subject to make your point clearer in the next parts.
Boy Does it need to be formal language? I mean, we are going to write our opinion on today's rap music after all…

Ms Crane Well, no, as long as you don't use slang … and don't forget: I want you to send them in via email by Thursday. And please, do NOT focus on a concert you've been to saying what you liked about it: that's not what I want.

Part 3 p. 19

Woman Hello, everyone. Welcome aboard the Sea Lady cruise liner. I'm Janet and I'm going to tell you about the beautiful cruise ship I work on as a stewardess. I'd like to give you a few facts about the ship before telling you what you can do during your cruise. The Sea Lady cruise ship was completed in 2014 and started its first tour of the Mediterranean in May 2015. It is 330 metres long and one of the top-20 largest ships in the world today; it can carry up to 2,500 passengers and 1,700 staff. On the Rainbow deck there are two pools and three hot tubs, two on the upper level and one on the lower level. It also has an area where you can place your deck chairs and sunbathe or relax near the pool during the day. You can use the same area to watch the beautiful music and light show when you have finished dinner. Dinner is served from seven fifteen to half past nine in three different dining rooms, where you can choose from Japanese, Italian or French cuisine. The music and light show starts at ten to ten every night so you will have plenty of time to reach the Rainbow deck after dinner. If you feel like a movie after the music and light show you can go to the Cloud 9 deck: it has one of the largest screens at sea and while guests enjoy the movie they can enjoy ice-cream, even fresh tropical fruit. If you are thirsty drinks are always available at the two cafeterias at the end of the deck. As the on-board cinema is very popular with guests I suggest you get there at least half an hour before the starting time at 10 to get a seat. Thanks for joining us on our tour of the Sea Lady and don't forget to visit us at www.whirlane.com: that's double U, double U, double U, dot, W-H-I-R-L-A-N-E dot COM.

Part 4 p. 20

Interviewer Today I'm here with the famous Japanese manga creator Masayoshi Uwai and I'm going to ask him a few question on his exciting job. How did you start drawing manga?

Masayoshi As long as I can remember, I've always been fond of drawing: I come from a poor family so we couldn't afford to own toys: my grandfather used to bring us manga that people threw away. I used to spend hours reading the stories and copying the drawings. Me and my sisters Kimiko and Emiko used to create our own characters and create new stories. They were just drawings but we actually played with them as if they were dolls living in a real place. Then I went to an art school: I had worked during my high school to save money for it, but I soon realised it wasn't suitable for me so I left the course after a couple of months and ended up teaching myself.

Interviewer How did you become a professional manga artist?

Masayoshi I had created a long story which got positive reviews from local editors so I decided to take part in a contest. I won first prize and in 1992 I officially started my career with 'Cherry Blossoms in the Snow'. It was an incredibly long series – about 45 volumes, so it wasn't always easy to develop the plot. I still remember it as one of the most enjoyable moments in my early career.

Interviewer And after that you wrote your masterpiece, 'Captain Pluto'?

Masayoshi Yes, that's right. Cherry Blossom was a very sad story, so I wanted to put some funny moments and adventure in my next series. That's how Captain Pluto was born. Cherry Blossom was mainly about the three sisters who had been separated at birth, but in Captain Pluto the focus was making people laugh with a lot of action too. Both the stories are set in ancient Japan, but there are more magic elements and fight scenes in Captain Pluto.

Interviewer How do you make your characters so lively?

Masayoshi Well, I'm getting older, but I still enjoy hanging out with my friends, until the early morning hours. So my friends inspired me to create the superhero family in Captain Pluto: I just tried to imagine what they would be like if they had magic powers. But although they look and behave like my friends, the supernatural features often come from Japanese folklore: for example, in the series my best friend, Boku, was found inside a giant peach as a baby as in the old folk tale Momotarou; and there are many other characters that remind you of old traditional stories from Japan.

Interviewer So why are your stories so popular in the West?

Masayoshi Well, I'm really glad to see so many manga fans in Europe and America. A few countries, like France for example, already have a long tradition for comics and that is definitely an advantage. Although the type of drawing is very different, manga are seen as Japanese pop culture so they are not just a form of children's entertainment. Besides, I noticed that now cosplay is very popular: people love dressing up as their favourite manga character. This probably comes from Japan where people have done this for a while.

Interviewer What is your advice to someone who wants to take up manga drawing?

Masayoshi The most important thing is creating an original story that develops in a way that nobody can predict. The best thing about Japanese manga stories is that they are often set in a world apart. It's pure imagination but at the same time the stories follow a complex structure so they are suitable for adult audiences too, especially those who are keen on science fiction.

Test 2

Part 1 p. 36

Rubric 1: How did the boy get to the appointment?
Girl Tony! You're late! Where have you been?
Boy Sorry I missed the bus. I was trying to decide whether to wait for the next bus or get a taxi when I saw my sister on her scooter across the street. Luckily she gave me a lift, because she works near here.
Girl What a coincidence! You were very lucky to meet her.
Boy Yes, I was, indeed: she also had a spare helmet with her.

Rubric 2: What time are they leaving for the concert?
Boy So, what are the plans for tomorrow's concert?
Girl The concert starts at eight forty-five but we should get there at half past eight. The coach leaves at a quarter to eight so I'll meet you in the school playground at half past seven. Don't be late, please!
Boy I won't. See you tomorrow!

Rubric 3: What's Mark doing this weekend?
Lucy Hi Mark, shall we go to the cinema on Saturday?
Mark Sorry, Lucy: I'm going to the mountains with my grandparents. I spent last weekend helping Mum to tidy up and clean the house, so I decided to take a break and enjoy myself: I love skiing. We can go to the cinema next weekend if you want.
Lucy OK then, we'll go next weekend! Have fun in the mountains!

Rubric 4: Which photograph are they going to send?
Boy Which picture do you want to send Laura?
Girl Oh, please not this one: I look horrible in it.
Boy But it's the only one with both of us standing in front of that amazing bridge.
Girl Why don't we send her this one: the tower is awesome, isn't it?
Boy Well, you're right: this one is better... All right then, shall we go and visit the old castle now?
Girl Sure, let's go.

Rubric 5: Where is the boy going on holiday?
Girl Where are you going on holiday this year? I'm going to Rome with my grandparents.
Boy Sounds great! I wish I could visit a historic city of Europe, too. Unfortunately, my sister is still too young I'm sure she'd get bored. Last year we spent a week on a farm by the lake and she really enjoyed it; that's why we've already booked a hotel at the seaside.

165

Transcripts

Rubric 6: What did Tracy forget to buy?
Dad Did you get all the things I wrote on the list, Tracy?
Tracy Yes, Dad. here's everything: bread, milk and cheese, That's all, I think. I didn't buy the eggs because there are already a dozen.
Dad Where's the lettuce? You know Mum only eats fruit and vegetables.
Tracy Oh, no...well... the shops are closed now, so I'll go and get some tomorrow: I guess she can have some strawberries and a banana for dinner.

Rubric 7: What will the weather be like on Thursday?
Gina Harry, have you heard about the weather for the weekend? They say it will rain!
Harry No, it won't: this weekend it will be sunny and warm again. The temperatures will be around twenty-two degrees for two days. But I don't expect this lovely weather to last, though: they say next week will begin with lower temperatures, with dry and cloudy days until Thursday, when we'll probably need our umbrella again.
Gina Oh, dear! I can't stand the rain anymore!

 Part 2 p. 38

Question 8
Daniel I've just finished my first lesson with Mr Watkins.
Lara Is that the new Science teacher? The tall one with short brown hair and glasses?
Daniel No, that's the Maths teacher: he's been in this school since I was in year one. Mr Watkins is quite young but he's bald. There he is! Can you see him? It's the guy talking to that middle-aged woman with short curly hair.

Question 9
Grandson So, Granny: what was it like when you were a child?
Grandma Well, we were very poor so we used to have meat very rarely, though I didn't really mind that since I never liked it very much. I remember on Christmas day my father took us to the restaurant and then we could order our favourite dishes. Mine was boiled beef and cabbage.
Grandson Poor you! I hate cabbage.
Grandma Actually, I've always loved this traditional Irish dish and I still do it when I invite my friends every time they ask me. I will never forget the roast potatoes my grandma used to make us, though. Unfortunately mine have never been as delicious as those. It's a pity she didn't teach me how to make them: I wish I could taste them again.

Question 10
Girl There it is! I thought it was in my pocket as usual.
Father Well, you are always leaving it everywhere. You should put it back in your wallet every time you use it. What was it doing on the desk near the remote control?
Girl I left it there when I got back from school: I was carrying my schoolbag so I forgot to put it back when I got off the bus.
Father Be careful, you may get a £20 fine if you don't have it when you travel.

Question 11
Teacher Our coach will stop in the village for a couple of hours, so you'll have time to visit the monument at the end of the road. There's also a street market in front of the monument with colourful stalls selling spices, handkerchiefs and other local handmade goods.
Boy Sounds great. It's my dad's birthday tomorrow and he's fond of cooking, so I'll get him some spices from the stalls!
Teacher Actually, I wouldn't suggest buying them there: they're quite expensive. Why don't you buy them at the little shop near the coach station?

Question 12
Girl Hello, I need some information.
Woman Sure, how can I help you?
Girl I'm a bit late and I'm afraid I'll miss my train to London. It will take too long to get to the station by bus: it only runs every 10 minutes...
Woman Well, the quickest way to the station is through the park: you'll have to walk round a little lake, but that way it'll take less than 10 minutes. When you get out of the park, go through the tunnel past the bus station and you'll reach platform 2. That's where all the trains to London stop. So you should get there in time to get on your train.
Girl Thank you!

Question 13
Lucas I'm so annoyed I missed class yesterday. What was Mrs Forster's lesson about?
Maggie It was about the effects of pollution and global warming.
Lucas Yeah, I know. Lots of animal and plant species will disappear unless we do something to stop destroying our planet.
Maggie Mrs Forster also said that the destruction of rainforests has also caused a lot of floods in many different geographical areas.
Lucas It sounds as a very interesting lesson.
Maggie Yes, it was.
Lucas And I'm very worried about our planet.
Maggie Me, too.

Part 3 p. 39

Woman Hello, everyone. I'm going to give you some information about our weekend hike before we leave tomorrow morning. Please, make notes as here are many things you must remember.
Our coach will be in front of the school's main entrance at 6.30 a.m.: I know it's really early, but do not be late as the journey's quite long. We're going to set out at a quarter to seven.
You mustn't bring more than one backpack because there isn't enough room on the coach and you don't need too much luggage anyway. We will provide for tents and meals for everybody, but don't forget to bring your own sleeping bags.
The weather forecast says it will be chilly until tomorrow night, so you need to pack warm clothes; however, it will be sunny on Sunday so bring your swimming things as you might need them when we get to the lake around midday. Please remember that we will spend most of our weekend hiking in the countryside so you don't need to bring too much money: 10 pounds will be enough for you to buy snacks and drinks when we stop in the little villages during our tour. Anyway, if you want, you can bring some extra money for Sunday afternoon: those who feel like shopping for souvenirs can take a bus to the nearest town, which is called Leavenworth and is 14 kilometres from the campsite. You can take the bus in front of the newsstand behind the campsite and get there in half an hour.
If you decide to go to Leavenworth remember you'll have to be back to the campsite by five thirty. You mustn't forget your mobile phones: if you have any problem you can text or ring me on 096775523.

Part 4 p. 40

Interviewer Today I am with Erika Mendel who has been a fashion blogger since 2018 when she became popular with her blog 'Think Pink'. So, Erika: can you first tell us who influences fashion trends in your opinion?
Erika Well, today's fashion industry is based on what journalists, stylists and celebrities like or not and new professional figures - such as bloggers, influencers and editors - have been created in recent years. However, it's not so easy to tell the difference between each role, but I think there is room for everybody.
Interviewer Erika, what is a blogger?
Erika Well, the easiest way to describe one is as someone who is well-known for their website: it might be photo-based or made up of written posts, but the common element is that in both types the viewers can understand what the blogger likes or dislikes. Fashion bloggers have a point of view and they present fashion in a personal way.
Interviewer Why do some bloggers lose popularity?

Erika	The most popular fashion bloggers and influencers have made a lot of money advertising products or supporting designer labels. However, the future of blogging is unsure – and some bloggers are closing their websites because they can't deal with competition from Instagram and other social media.
Interviewer	Erika, can you tell us something about teen influencers?
Erika	Influencers are slightly different from bloggers: they don't always have blogs and they typically work on social media. They're paid to attend fashion shows, events and parties because fashion companies want to have them there. Today a teen influencer's popularity depends on how many followers they have; however, the followers must be between 12 to 20 years old. Fashion companies pay teen influencers to wear their clothes on social media.
Interviewer	Finally, Erika, could you tell us about editors: who are they?
Erika	Editors are easier to define than bloggers and influencers. A fashion editor has to describe the fashion industry according to a magazine's ideas on the subject. They might write articles about new trends or the people like models or popular celebrities. In the past editors used to hold the front row positions, but they are now as important as influencers and bloggers. A fashion editor can work freelance or work for a single magazine or newspaper.

Test 3

Part 1 p. 56

Rubric 1: Where did she leave the keys?

Mum	I can't find my keys anywhere. Do you know where they are, Kevin?
Kevin	No, Mum, I haven't seen them. Don't you usually keep them in your bag?
Woman	Usually, but I've looked there.
Kevin	Ah – hang on. Are those your keys, on the table?
Woman	Did you say under the table?
Kevin	No mum! On the table, between the telephone and those old pencils!
Woman	Ah yes, here they are! Thanks Kevin, you're wonderful!

Rubric 2: How did she get to school?

Girl	Well, I'm never doing that again!
Boy	What's the matter?
Girl	You know I always come to school by bus? Well, the bus was delayed today ….
Boy	Mmm…?
Girl	So, I thought it would be a good idea to walk. My brother offered to drive me here but I don't like using the car if possible. But it's much further to school than I thought! And I'm wearing new shoes and now my feet hurt!
Boy	Oh dear. Maybe next time you should accept your brother's offer!

Rubric 3: Where is the supermarket?

Dad	Suzie, can you go to the new supermarket for me and pick up some food for lunch?
Girl	New supermarket? Where's that?
Dad	You know, along the High Street, opposite the garages.
Girl	Oh, that's really far away, Dad! Can't you drive there?
Dad	No, there's only a small car park in front of it. There's no space to park.
Girl	Why didn't they build a supermarket on the corner! There's a lot more space for cars there….

Rubric 4: What was the weather like yesterday?

Woman	Well, the good news for everyone is that tomorrow's weather looks very good. There will be a lot of sunshine for most of us, which will be a change from the terrible wind and rain we've had today. So, get your sunglasses out, because tomorrow's weather will be the same as it was yesterday – so you can start making your plans!

Rubric 5: What are they going to give their daughter?

Man	It's Claire's birthday next week, what shall we get her?
Woman	Oh, the same as Colin, a new jacket!
Man	Really? That's not going to be very exciting for her.
Woman	But she loves clothes! As long as it's the latest fashion, she'll be happy.
Man	Why don't we get her a jacket and matching boots?
Woman	Yes, why not? She'd be pleased with that. Not white, though: they'll get dirty.

Rubric 6: What date is her aunt coming?

Girl	Dad, what date are we going on holiday?
Dad	Well, I'm very busy at work at the moment. I'm free from the 20th, so we'll go then.
Girl	Oh! That's the same day as Aunty Helen's coming! Remember? To look after the house while we're away.
Dad	Are you sure that's right? She's coming on the 18th, isn't she?
Girl	Hold on, I'll go and check in my diary! … Ah! No, we're both wrong! It's the 19th. That's strange! I was sure it was the 18th…

Rubric 7: What ingredients does the boy need to get?

Boy	Mum, I've got my cookery class tomorrow. Have we got all the ingredients I need?
Mum	I bought some eggs and flour yesterday and of course we've got salt and pepper.
Boy	I need some cheese, tomatoes and slices of meat too.
Mum	Let me check in the fridge … Well, we've got some tomatoes but we haven't got any cheese or meat left.
Boy	But I need them for tomorrow!
Mum	Well, don't worry, the shop is five minutes away, so why don't you go and pick them up now?
Boy	OK ……..

Part 2 p. 58

Question 8

Girl	So, it's your birthday on Saturday! Do you know what your parents are giving you?
Boy	No, I don't know yet! Mum said she wants it to be a surprise! I asked for a new digital camera.
Girl	Oh, that's a good idea. What else did you ask for?
Boy	Well, I'd really like a new bike, but unfortunately I think that's too expensive. Actually, I think mum's organising a trip somewhere.
Girl	Really? Why do you think that?
Boy	Well my little sister said that this time next week I'll be relaxing on a beach.
Girl	Wow! That sounds great!
Boy	Yeah, but not so great if my sister's coming too!

Question 9

Girl	So, what time's the flight again, Mum?
Mum	Well, it was supposed to leave at twelve thirty, but I've checked on the website, and now it says it's going to take off four hours later, at half past four!
Girl	Oh no, how annoying! But, on the other hand, it means we have time for lunch here now.
Mum	Yes, that sounds like a good idea. I'll make something now. And then let's finish packing our bags!
Girl	Well you can, but I don't need to. I packed mine last night. I'm ready to go!

Question 10

Girl	So how was Maria's party, Oliver?
Boy	It was OK, I suppose. The music was quite good but too loud for me. But everyone danced. It was… great.
Girl	You don't sound very sure!
Boy	No, no it was fine. There was lots of delicious food and …
Girl	Come on Oliver! I can tell that something's wrong. Didn't you have a good time?
Boy	Well, no, not really. It wasn't the actual party, but the people. There were a few that I didn't really want to see…
Girl	Oh no! Now I understand why you didn't have a good time. Poor you!

Transcripts

Question 11
- **Man** Hello, how can I help you?
- **Girl** Hi, I'd like to buy a return ticket to Brighton, please.
- **Man** When are you travelling back?
- **Girl** I'm not exactly sure, maybe next Monday.
- **Man** Well, an open return is £67. That means you can come back any time before the end of next month. Or, the best value is a fixed return but you must come back next Monday. That's only £43.50. I would buy that ticket if you can. But you know, a single to Brighton is just £25… two singles are cheaper than the open return.
- **Girl** Yes, it's more expensive than the fixed return… Hmmm, OK, I'll get the £43.50 one and make sure I come back on Monday.

Question 12
- **Asst** Hello, can I help you?
- **Girl** Yes, I'm looking for a top to go with this skirt. Nothing too casual.
- **Asst** I see. What about this blouse?
- **Girl** That's nice and smart, but it's a bit dark. Have you got anything lighter?
- **Asst** Yes, of course. How about this?
- **Girl** Yes, I prefer that colour, but it looks too big. Have you got it in a smaller size?
- **Asst** Why not try it on first? These blouses look better when they are a bit loose.
- **Girl** Yes, OK. Where's the changing room?

Question 13
- **Boy** Emily, can you help me with this homework?
- **Girl** I'm quite busy at the moment, but, OK, if it doesn't take long …
- **Boy** Thanks! Look, it's exercises four to eight.
- **Girl** OK, so what have you done so far?
- **Boy** Well, I started exercise four, but it didn't work so I gave up …
- **Girl** You mean you haven't even tried! Come on, Dan! I don't understand why you can't do them. These are easy!
- **Boy** Yeah, but you're so much quicker than me.
- **Girl** Look, Dan, I've got my own homework to do. I'm not doing yours for you just because you can't be bothered!

Part 3 p. 59

Man Good morning! I'm very glad to see so many of you here today to join our trip to the Country Show and Fair. There are so many things to do that I can only tell you about the main attractions; you'll have to discover all the rest for yourselves!
First, let me remind you that the show opens in about five minutes' time, at nine o'clock, and closes at 7 p.m. You must leave before the main entrance is locked. The most interesting thing about the show, in my opinion, is the wide range of hand-made products on sale. The prices can be high, but if you go to the north section of the show area you will find the cheapest goods. Naturally, the children will be keen to go to the funfair, and we have a special offer on at the moment: if you buy a green all-day ticket, access to all the rides and attractions is included in the price! The ticket costs ten pounds, but I am sure you will find it a very good buy in the end.
There is usually a very good fruit and vegetable competition in the enormous tent in the middle of the showground at three thirty each afternoon. Another particularly fun thing about the show is the traditional sports and games which take place at one o'clock and last for at least two hours. Well, I hope you find plenty of things to do. Don't get lost, and ask the security people dressed in yellow if you need anything. We'll meet back here by the bus at a quarter past …

Part 4 p. 60

- **Man** Hi Katie. It's a pleasure to have you here. I love eating, and I'm a huge fan of your show. But I must admit that I am not the most skilled cook. In fact, I almost need a recipe for boiling water!
- **Katie** You may not believe it, but many of the people who watch my show are just like you; they don't have much cooking experience, but they like to watch because they love a good meal and want to learn to make one themselves.
- **Man** Well, that definitely describes me. My problem, to be quite honest, is that I am a bit nervous about cooking.
- **Katie** That doesn't surprise me. Many of my fans have said that they are afraid of making mistakes when they prepare a meal. But I also believe that some people who watch my programme for the first time and some also think that cooking good food takes a long time. They think you only get good food in restaurants! After seeing my show, I hope they realize that they were wrong about that.
- **Man** That's another reason why I like your show; your recipes are simple and fast. Another problem I have is that I am almost too busy to go shopping for ingredients. I manage to go shopping maybe once a week, or even less often, so I usually just buy lots of frozen dinners and tins of food.
- **Katie** It's true that some ingredients, such as fresh fish, should be used soon after you buy them. But there are many things that you can keep for a long time, such as rice, pasta, carrots, onions, olive oil, cheese, salt and pepper … maybe some frozen peas or tinned tomatoes… potatoes… It's amazing how many delicious dishes you can make with those things.
- **Man** What would you tell someone who says that they can't afford to buy the right equipment for cooking?
- **Katie** That's just not true. My mother – who taught me so much about cooking – always used the cheapest pots and pans that she could find, and she never made a dish I didn't like.
- **Man** So, how can I get started cooking? As I said before, I'm a bit nervous about…
- **Katie** Look, cooking is almost as natural as eating. Anyone can do it if they try. You need to stop making excuses and just start doing it. And remember that mistakes are also opportunities to learn something.

Test 4

Part 1 p. 76

Rubric 1: What is the girl going to have for dinner?
- **Dad** What shall we have for dinner, Grace?
- **Grace** I don't know, Dad. I had a piece of cake and some tea an hour ago so I'm not so hungry now.
- **Dad** How about ordering pizza?
- **Grace** Mmmmm, you know I love pizza – I could eat pizza every day! – but I think I'll just have some fruit salad this evening. What are you going to eat?
- **Dad** Well, I'll make a couple of hamburgers and chips. and maybe I'll have a little fruit, too.

Rubric 2: Which souvenir does the boy decide to buy?
- **Tom** I mustn't forget to get a souvenir for my sister Sally.
- **Eddie** This black T-shirt with the Eiffel Tower's lovely, isn't it? I think she might like it.
- **Tom** Yeah, but she has loads of T-shirts and I wanted something more interesting. Do you think she'd like this scarf?
- **Eddie** Ugh! It's awful! Look: I got my sister this French perfume. Maybe you could get one for Sally, too.
- **Tom** I don't know. I guess she'll get the usual T-shirt: she wears them all the time, so she'll probably enjoy having one from Paris.

Rubric 3: Where is Dave calling from?
- **Mum** Hi Dave. Is everything all right?
- **Boy** Hi, Mum. I'm afraid I missed the train back home. I was chatting with my coach at the football pitch when I realised it was late. I ran as fast as I could but I couldn't make it in time. Could you pick me up from the coach station when you leave the office? I'll be in front of the main entrance at 5.30.
- **Mum** OK, don't worry. I'll pick you up.
- **Boy** Thanks Mum!

Rubric 4: Which building is the museum?
- **Boy** Excuse me, could you tell me the way to the town hall from here?
- **Man** Sure. It's not far so you can walk there. Just go past the hospital and take the first on the left.
- **Boy** Is the hospital the building with the stone statue outside the front door?

168

Man	No, that's the History Museum. The hospital is the tall building over there. When you turn left you'll see the town hall with a flag above the entrance. You can't miss it.
Boy	Thank you.

Rubric 5: How much did Adam pay for the computer game?

Adam	I can't wait to play this game!
Matt	You bought it?! I thought you said it was too expensive.
Adam	Well, actually, I couldn't spend 50 pounds on a game, but last week there was a 40% discount at the shop I always go to and they took it down to 30 pounds, so I got it.
Matt	That's great.
Adam	Why don't you come over this afternoon so we can try it?
Matt	Sure, see you later then.

Rubric 6: What did Carol's mother use to do?

Luke	Hi, Carol. How's your mother's new job at the bakery's?
Carol	It's great. She says she really loves the smell of the bread as she gets it out of the oven. The morning is the busiest time: they get calls from restaurant owners ordering bread or cakes that must be delivered before lunchtime.
Luke	Well, I guess it's much more fun than sitting at a desk and staring at a computer all day. I'm sure she doesn't miss working at the office, does she?
Carol	No, that's for sure.

Rubric 7: Which pet would the girl like to get?

Adele	Aww, the little white one in the corner of the cage is so cute. Can we get it, Mum?
Mum	I don't know, Adele. Our cat Toby might not like it.
Adele	But my friend Emma says there are no problems with her pets: she has a rabbit, a dog and a cat and they all get on well.
Mum	Ok, let's buy it. We'll need to get some food too, though. What do rabbits eat?
Adele	I know they eat carrots, but I think we should ask the pet shop assistant: she'll suggest the best food for it.

 **Part 2 p. 78**

Question 8

Boy	Have you met Lisa, the new librarian?
Girl	Yes, she seems to be doing well, doesn't she?
Boy	Well, I must admit that when she started last week I thought she would find it a bit difficult to organise things because she's so young.
Girl	I like her... She's hard-working and she's going to learn fast, I'm sure.
Boy	Yeah, that's right. Besides you need a bit of experience to do this job, whatever your age.

Question 9

Girl	Hey, Tony. Is this your new smartphone?
Boy	Yeah (*disappointed voice*)... I have to take it back to the store.
Girl	What? But you got it yesterday!
Boy	I know... I downloaded a few songs because I wanted to try the headphones but I could hardly hear a thing. I borrowed my sister's earphones to check if mine were broken, but it was just the same. I'm pretty sure it's the volume button: it's stuck down and it won't move up. What a disappointment!

Question 10

Lara	Hi, Sally. I'm calling because I might be a bit late for our basketball practice at three this afternoon. I was supposed to go to the dentist this morning but her secretary called and asked if we could put it off to quarter to three. So I was wondering if we could meet half an hour later and then go to the basketball practice as usual.
Sally	No worries, Lara. I'll meet you at half past three then.
Lara	OK, Sally, thank you. See you later!

Question 11

Lewis	Did you get anything from the shopping centre?
Fiona	Well, I really wanted to get a bottle of shampoo my uncle gave me a few months ago because I really love its smell and I'm running out of it; but then I remembered my dad got a spare bottle last week so it wasn't really necessary. Anyway I got Mark the video game he wanted and look what I got for you!
Lewis	Oh, this is the DVD I wanted to buy last week! Thank you, Fiona!
Fiona	You're welcome Lewis. And happy birthday!

Question 12

Boy	So, Miss Turner, is this where we're coming later?
Miss Turner	Yes. We'll meet back here in about two hours. As you can see the entrance is over there: when you get in you'll see that it's in the shape of a large ring on the three levels. There is no roof in the middle, so if you were richer you could sit in the seats around the edge, while the poorer people stood on the floor around the stage, which was over a meter high to allow everybody to see the play. Unlike today the audience was very loud and often threw things on the stage if they didn't like the play.
Boy	Wow, I didn't know that! Thank you Miss Turner.

Question 13

Woman	Hi Tellisha. We're very happy to have you here today. Could you tell us about your life as a young gymnast?
Girl	I've been a gymnast for 8 years and I really enjoy being on this team. I get on well with all the other girls: we're all friends and we often have dinner together, though we have to follow a special diet to keep us strong and fit. And of course unless you keep working hard, you won't improve.
Woman	It sounds very challenging! Is there anything you find very hard in your everyday life?
Girl	Well, since you must train almost every day, you have very little time to do other things you like so you also need to be well-organised.

Part 3 p. 79

Man	Are you writing a short story for our next fiction competition? As it's the 10th of March, there are just five weeks to go until the closing date of the 15th of April. The best story will be selected on May 2nd to be published in this year's collection. Sometimes writers entering contests think that if there is a word limit, they need to write to the maximum word count permitted. For this competition, that's 10,000 words, but you don't need to write up this much. There is no lower limit, which means you could write as few as 500 words and still be considered. However, If you're more interested in writing a short story, we would recommend you enter our sister competition, the Stratford Flash Fiction Competition, which is for stories of 3,000 words and under. As I said before though, don't worry: you may be selected to be published in the winner's anthology even though your story is very short: last year's best story 'Mind if I join you?' by young Danish writer Agnes Jepsen, was just 4,500 words long. You can buy our past years' story collections from our website www.novelsnpoems.com in hard copy, while this year's will also be available in digital versions from major online stores, too: if you buy it from our website, however, you'll only have to pay 8 pounds 50 as there will be a 30% discount.

Part 4 p. 80

Interviewer	Good morning Lenny, you've been a Mandarin teacher for over 2 years now. Can you tell me how you decided to take up teaching?
Lenny	Well, I had a degree in business studies and the first job I was offered was in an accounting firm. I'd never considered taking advantage of the fact I was a native Mandarin speaker for work. It happened by chance one evening, while I was at a Chinese restaurant with my girlfriend and a few of her friends: one of them owned a language school, and she was looking for someone to teach Chinese classes to her students. So that's how it all started.
Interviewer	Mandarin is often considered a very hard language to learn. Do you agree?

169

Transcripts

Lenny	Well, it depends. Compared to English Chinese grammar is actually quite simple and there aren't as many rules as in most Western languages. The real challenge is pronunciation, since Chinese has 5 different stresses for each word and most people can't tell the difference between sounds. As for vocabulary, I've found a way to help them memorise new words by using fixed phrases.
Interviewer	Lenny, what do you usually teach your students when they start learning Chinese?
Lenny	Beginner students must become familiar with the sounds of Mandarin, so I usually spend the first few lessons explaining that there are five different stresses: the meaning of words depends on how you pronounce them. Of course you need a lot of practice: you need to listen and speak in class, with a teacher checking what you say all the time.
Interviewer	How about Chinese characters: are they as hard to learn as they look?
Lenny	Well, yes. They are very difficult to learn for native speakers as well. What I focus on, however, is reading rather than writing. Whenever I can, I show my students that characters are often drawings representing things: when they see the thing in the drawing they usually find it easier to recognise their shape, so they can learn as many as a hundred characters in a few months.
Interviewer	How can Mandarin students improve their learning?
Lenny	I think that when you learn a language, your vocabulary makes a difference. Watching subtitled movies or reading magazines and papers is great of course, but you can get better results if you try to learn from 5 to 8 words a day. Believe me: it works wonders after just a couple of months.
Interviewer	So Lenny, will you work as a Mandarin teacher in the future?
Lenny	Definitely! But I feel I must be qualified: I've been on a Teacher Training course at university and I'm going to get my degree next year. I've already applied to several schools and they're all very interested. I'd like to write a Mandarin language book but I guess it will take a while before I can do that.

Test 5

 **Part 1 p. 96**

Rubric 1: What is she wearing?
Dad Oh! You've got changed. Are you going somewhere?
Girl Yes, Dad! It's the school party tonight and I'm thinking of wearing this. What do you think?
Dad Well the jacket's very nice, and the skirt is all right. But don't you think that belt's rather thick and heavy?
Girl Hmmm, yes, I see what you mean. It doesn't go with this light skirt. Perhaps a thin one would be better.
Dad Well, why don't you go and try?
Girl Yes, good idea!

Rubric 2: Where is the clock?
Boy Oh no …. It looks like Aunt Meg has moved all the sitting room furniture again!
Girl Oh yes. Wasn't the clock between the shelves and the mirror before?
Boy No, there's no space there for a clock there! I think it used to be above the mirror.
Girl Oh yes, you're right. Now it's up there, above the shelves.
Boy She probably put it there so we can't look at it while eating!
Girl Ha ha! Yes, probably!

Rubric 3: What arrived in the post today?
Mum Well, well, it's your lucky day!
Boy Really?! Why's that?
Mum The post has come. There's a postcard for you, and a parcel.
Boy Isn't there anything else? I'm expecting a letter from Sandra. Is that it?
Mum No, sorry! There's just the postcard, parcel, oh, and a couple of letters.
Boy For me? They don't look very interesting ….
Mum No, they're for me and they're probably just a couple of bills.

Rubric 4: Which picture do they like?
Girl Hmm...this gallery isn't very good! I don't like many of the pictures!
Boy Yeah! You see that one with the castle in it. It's awful!
Girl Ha, yes, and look at the countryside in the background. It's terrible! I could paint better than that! What do you think of the flowers in the vase?
Boy Well, they're not bad at all, better than the painting of the old woman!
Girl Yes, you're right!

Rubric 5: What does she want for her birthday?
Boy Well, it's not long until the big day, Alice. What would you like to get this year?
Girl I really hope I don't get the same as last year.
Boy Why? What did you get then?
Girl Some books but they weren't very interesting. I'd be pleased with some jewellery.
Boy Didn't you get some clothes last year too?
Girl Oh yes, I forgot! But I want something different this year.
Boy Well, you'll see on your birthday!

Rubric 6: What hobby will he try next?
Girl So, are you going to join another club, Samuel?
Boy Well, I'm always looking for something new to do in my spare time.
Girl You're good at art, have you thought about painting?
Boy Yes, I've considered it, but I think I'd like to do something that helps to keep me fit. I've thought about skiing but that's probably too expensive, to be honest. I think I'll take up swimming, though.
Girl That makes sense. Then maybe you can do some painting next year.

Rubric 7: Which one is Uncle Jake?
Girl Look! Have you seen these old photographs? They're amazing!
Boy Yes, look at that one! Dad with his long hair and beard! I think he looked terrible!
Girl I know, he looks funny. At least his hair was still dark then.
Boy Let's be honest, Uncle Jake wasn't much better! He had long hair too!
Girl And a moustache! And then there's Fred. I wonder why his hair wasn't long too. Long hair was the fashion.
Boy Maybe but was the only tidy one!

Part 2 p. 98
Question 8
Doc. Hello Sam, what seems to be the trouble?
Boy Well, I've got a really bad cold and a headache.
Doc. I see. And how long have you been feeling like this?
Boy Well, the headache only started yesterday, but I've had a cold for a week. I didn't go to school for the last two days and my mum made me stay in bed, but I still don't feel any better.
Doc. OK, let's have a look at you...

Question 9
Girl So did you have a good weekend, Dan?
Boy It was OK. I went to the cinema with my friends on Sunday afternoon.
Girl Really? What did you see?
Boy The new Shadowhunters film. I thought it was pretty cool.
Girl That's funny! I saw that on Sunday, too, but I didn't see you at the cinema. Was it the 3 o'clock showing?
Boy Yes, but we got there a bit late and sat at the back of the cinema.
Girl Well, I was at the back of the Odeon, too. How strange!
Boy Ah, that explains it, Lizzie. I saw it at the Plaza. That's why we didn't see each other!

Question 10
Boy How was your holiday at the water sports centre? Did you go windsurfing?
Girl Yes, I did. I found that the windsurfing course I did last year was a big help because I could go straight out on the water. I tried sailing too, but I didn't really like it.

170

Boy	Why not? I love sailing.
Girl	Well, I expected it to be more exciting, but you spend most of your time just sitting in a boat ...
Boy	Hmmm, I don't think that's quite true, Julia! Anyway, did you do any other water sports?
Girl	Well, lots of people were having lessons in waterskiing, but I didn't have enough time for that. I preferred to spend the week just windsurfing in the end, to be honest.

Question 11

Girl	Look at these shoes, Ben. Do you like them? Are the heels too high?
Boy	I think the heels are OK, but I don't really like the colour. They are a bit boring: too much like school shoes. What about these silver ones?
Girl	Ben! Are you crazy? I can't go to the party in silver shoes! But you're right about the colour of the others. Oh dear, this is really annoying. Mum says that if I don't find something today, I'll have to wear the shoes I had at my sister's wedding...
Boy	Well, what about those blue ones over there?
Girl	Wow! I totally love those ones! You're brilliant, Ben!

Question 12

Girl	Is that a photo of your new dog, Jim? He's so sweet!
Boy	Yeah, this is Zorro. He's a bit crazy!
Girl	Actually, I think he looks a lot like your old dog.
Boy	Hmmm, maybe he looks similar in this photo, but Zorro's a lot bigger than Jasper was, and he's much friendlier. But I miss Jasper, of course. He wasn't very friendly and he was much lazier than Zorro, but for me he was the best dog ever!

Question 13

Boy	So have you thought about what you'll do when you leave school yet, Jessie?
Girl	No, not really. I suppose I'll go to university, but I don't know what to study and I really don't know what job I'll end up doing. I'd quite like to work with animals, but I really hate biology so I can't be a vet like my dad... What about you, Harry? What will you do?
Boy	Well, I want to do a gap year before university, then I'm going to study medicine. Both of my parents are doctors and it's such an important job. I hope that one day I'll do that too.

Part 3 p. 99

Man	And for those of you who love the cinema, mark your calendars for this year's film festival in Slotherington. Once a year for twelve days, this small town fills up with film enthusiasts from all over Britain, as well as from other parts of the world. Last year, there were over eighty films shown, and this year, there are over a hundred planned. From the time the first film was shown almost five years ago, organisers of this festival have always used the word 'variety' when describing the event. This year, the word International has also been added to the name of the festival because each year more and more of the films being shown at the festival come from other countries. In fact, last year's biggest hit was called *Feilding* by the young New Zealand director, Zoe Mayer. The film is set in the town of that name. We're showing it again this year! Feilding, that's F-E-I-L-D-I-N-G. Don't miss it! This year is the fifth anniversary of the festival. It opens on the first of July. Tickets for each film are only £4.50, but it's possible to see up to 6 films per day, so if you can spend the entire day watching films, a one-day ticket, at £19.50, is much better value. If you are planning on spending more than three days at the festival, you should buy the festival pass for £50. And if there are any young people listening, you might want to come along since there is a new film category this year: Films for Children. If you are interested in films, this is one of the best events of the year, and I definitely recommend it. For information on the films that will be shown, you can go to the official festival website at www dot...

Part 4 p. 100

Man	Now, you might remember last month we announced the winner of our Young Travel Reporter competition. Well, that winner, Maggie Johnston, has been sent off to Somerford where we can join her now. Hello Maggie! How does it feel to be on the road, so to speak?
Maggie	Great! I'm having lots of fun here in Somerford.
Man	What can you tell us about it?
Maggie	Well, it is a fascinating place to visit and offers lots to do for everyone but – more importantly! – lots for us teen travellers! The city is very well organised for tourists, with an information centre in the station so that you can get maps and help with hotels as soon as you arrive if you come by train. You can hire bikes here if you want to race around the city on two wheels.
Man	So, what's there to do?
Maggie	There're plenty of things to do! In the city centre the main attraction is the 14th century castle, which is almost exactly the same as it was 600 hundred years ago. The only recent changes are the roofs, which were repaired last year, and the entrance. But the original walls and towers are great. I loved the castle tour in particular, because all the guides are trained entertainers. History comes alive and is nothing like those boring lessons at school!
Man	Anywhere else worth seeing?
Maggie	The old university. Don't ask where it is, because it's all around you, like in Oxford or Cambridge. Almost every old building seems to belong to one department or another. The oldest building in the whole place, Bernard's Tower, is now the science library's home. But it's not all about the past here in Somerford. The new Eastfield shopping centre has over 150 different stores and cafés. And just north of the city centre, there's also a wonderful park. It's full of rides and activities and beautiful landscaped grassy areas for tired old parents to relax in, ha ha!
Man	So, all sounds perfect then?
Maggie	Well, maybe for a day trip. But if you want to spend the night in Somerford, I have to say you might be disappointed. There are very few hotels here, and they are not very modern, and not cheap at all! So take lots of money with you! There is a campsite outside the town, but who wants to be in a tent in the British rain? But I'm having a fantastic two days in Somerford and would definitely come back again.
Man	Ok, thanks Maggie, we'll catch you on your next trip..... Now, have you ever thought about ...

Test 6

Part 1 p. 116

Rubric 1: Where were the girls supposed to meet?

Mia	Kaylee, this is Mia. Where are you?! We were supposed to meet at the café next to the school to go to the club together. What happened?
Kaylee	Hi, Mia. Actually I'm waiting for you at home. This afternoon there's no workshop because the teacher is sick. Don't you remember I texted you yesterday? We had planned to do our Maths homework together...
Mia	Oh, yeah... you're right, I'm sorry Kaylee: I had completely forgotten. I'll be there in about 15 minutes. See you there.

Rubric 2: What time will the train leave?

Man	This is an announcement for all passengers travelling on the 11.35 train to Leeds. We regret to inform you that due to problems on the railway line, this train has been delayed by forty minutes. The new departure time will be at quarter past twelve. Please check the departures board for the platform where the train will leave from. We apologise for any difficulty this may cause you. Thank you.

Rubric 3: Which dress does the girl want to wear?

Girl	Mum, can you get me the white dress? It's in the wardrobe upstairs.
Mum	Is it the one with short sleeves and a blue belt?
Girl	No, I mean the one with a dark collar and 3 buttons on the front. I think it's next to the blouse with flowers I wore to Amy's party last Saturday.
Mum	Ok, I found it. I'll bring it downstairs in a minute.

171

Transcripts

Rubric 4: Which sport does the girl want to take up?
Tony Hi, Helen. Did you enjoy your holiday in Italy?
Helen It was absolutely fantastic. I did a lot of swimming and scuba diving – you know I'm really into water sports. And I did yoga every morning. Now that I've tried it I want to join a course: it really helps you to relax. And my brother and I went horse-riding every day… it was such a great week. I wish holidays were longer…

Rubric 5: Where is the boy going first after school?
Brad Hi Ted. Are you and Pete going straight from school to the football pitch today?
Ted Actually, I'm leaving school a bit earlier today.
Brad Oh. Are you not playing football today then?
Ted Of course! I'm leaving early because I need to go to the dentist. I'm meeting Pete after that, outside the shopping centre. He doesn't know where the pitch is as he's never played with us.
Brad Ok then, I'll see you at the shopping centre with Pete, too.

Rubric 6: What will Emma do this Sunday?
Pete Hi Emma, what are you doing this Saturday?
Emma Hi Pete, I was supposed to go to a workshop on cooking, you know I love it, but my uncle has just asked me if I can help him at the shop. The girl who works for him is sick.
Pete Oh, too bad. I was going to ask you to go shopping together. We need to get something for Beatrix. It's her birthday next Thursday.
Emma Don't worry about that, I know she wanted to buy a pair of jeans she saw online last week. I'll get them on Sunday evening when I get back from my tennis match.

Rubric 7: What does the boy decide to buy for his niece?
Sales assistant Good afternoon, can I help you?
Boy Yes, er… I need to get a birthday present for my niece, but I have no idea what to get a 5-year-old girl.
Sales assistant How about this teddy bear: children that age usually love soft toys.
Boy Uhm, yeah… I guess so, but I think she's got loads of them already, so I was thinking of a puzzle or something creative. My aunt says she enjoys painting.
Sales assistant We've got these easy 50-piece animal puzzles, but I'd give an artistic girl a drawing kit. How about this one? It includes a colouring booklet and pencils too.
Boy Sounds like a great idea. I'll take it.

 **Part 2 p. 118**

Question 8
Jane Hi Chris, I hear your mum's been promoted. So, you'll have to move to Montreal, right?
Chris Yes, that's right.
Jane How do you feel about leaving here?
Chris Actually, I don't mind living in a different city, but I'm a bit nervous as I'll be starting a new school and I've no idea what the teachers or other students will be like.
Jane Don't you have to take a French test, too?
Chris Yes, sure, but that doesn't bother me: as you know my Mum's from Québec and she always talks to me in French anyway.

Question 9
Boy So what do you feel like watching?
Girl What are the options?
Boy Well, how about watching the film about that boy who became a F1 world champion before he was 20, or the latest season of your favourite series or the Oscar-winning zombie film? I can't remember the title but they say it's great!
Girl Ugh, no! I hate zombies! I know you find them thrilling but they really scare me. And I've already seen all the episodes of the series…
Boy Ok, let's watch the sports film then.
Girl Boring! Why don't we watch the cooking reality show?

Question 10
Mother Luke, I see you've tidied your room…and about time. Why did it take you so long?
Luke Mum, you know I had to finish cutting the grass first. I had promised Dad that I'd do that yesterday but it was raining so I had to do it today.
Mother OK, OK. well, I'll start making dinner now. By the way, could you just get a few things at the shop? I need eggs, milk and…
Luke Oh come on, can't you ask Lisa? She hasn't done anything today!
Mother Lisa's preparing for her test tomorrow. Stop complaining and go!

Question 11
Boy So, this was your first time ice-skating. How did you like it?
Girl I couldn't wait to try and I thought it'd be harder to learn, but I wish I had put on my gloves. I had no idea it'd be so cold on the rink.
Boy Well, that's normal. At least we didn't have to wait to get in.
Girl Of course there was no queue: I'm sure there are very few people our age who can afford it. I could only get in because my aunt gave me some extra pocket money for my birthday…
Boy But you had a great time, didn't you?
Girl Sure I did, but I won't be able to come back until I turn 15 next year.

Question 12
Girl Hi, Rob. Your sister told me your dance school show was brilliant.
Boy Well, that's what everybody says. Actually, I'm glad it's over. I don't know, I think I was a bit nervous, so it definitely wasn't my best performance. And it was the first time I had to dance with a mask on my face.
Girl It must be annoying…
Boy It is indeed, the thing is I couldn't see anything when the lights were down in the first five minutes. Well, luckily I don't think I'll have to dance in front of an audience again for a while.

Question 13
Girl Hey Jack. Are you still on the school volleyball team?
Boy Actually, I quit last summer. After 5 years it's time for me to take up a new sport…
Girl Are you serious? But you loved it!
Boy I did and I still do, but I didn't get along with the new coach. Besides, two of my best friends had already left the team, so it wasn't so hard to give it up.
Girl I guess now you'll have more time to go cycling with me, won't you?
Boy Sure, and I think it's more fun to do sports outside. In fact, I was thinking we could go for a ride tomorrow.
Girl Sounds great.

Part 3 p. 119
Man Ok, listen everyone. Our trip to Stratford is tomorrow: please remember that we're meeting in front of the station at a quarter to nine as our train is at a five past nine so do not be late. The journey will only last half an hour and a coach will pick us up from Stratford station when we get there at nine thirty-five. The first place we'll visit from ten to eleven is where Anne Hathaway, William Shakespeare's wife, lived as a girl. This lovely cottage will show you what people's everyday life was like 500 years ago, as this is when the cottage was built. From Anne Hathaway's cottage we'll go to the Stratford Butterfly Farm which is just a short walk. Our visit around the farm will start at quarter past eleven in the large greenhouse. There's usually a collection of spiders and insects in the greenhouse, but unfortunately the area where they are kept is closed tomorrow. Anyway, the greenhouse also has a beautiful waterfall that you'll see when you walk around.
We'll leave the farm at around midday and start our Stratford town walk with a local guide who will tell us about the history of Shakespeare's hometown. The guide will take us to the Avon river and there we'll stop to have lunch in the Avon bank gardens from around 1 p.m. to half past two p.m.

172

Our afternoon activity will be visiting the house where Shakespeare was born, now the Shakespeare Birthplace Trust. The tour of the house will last one and a half hours. When the tour's over, we'll have time to buy souvenirs. Don't forget to bring along your mobile phones as you may need it during the tour. Stratford isn't a big town but you may get lost, so in case that happens write down my number. It's 07881 243972. OK, if you have any questions now…

🔊 24 Part 4 p. 120

Man Today we are going to interview Amrita Bakshi, who is the youngest computer programmer in the world. Amrita, when did you first become interested in computers?

Amrita Well, my father is a software developer so he was obviously an important influence on me. However, my earliest memory of solving a computer problem was in preschool, when I was around five years old. I remember I wanted to use a computer and my teacher told me that it was out of order. Nobody could understand what was wrong with it. Well, I quickly fixed it when I saw that the power cable wasn't plugged in! That's when I realised I wanted to learn more about computers and machines in general.

Man And then you created your first program, right?

Amrita Yes, well… Actually, the first program I built wasn't for computers. It was an app, a program which works on smartphones or tablets. I started working on it when I was seven. It was called Verb-App and it helped foreign students of English to learn the spelling and pronunciation of irregular verbs. I was only 9 when my app was accepted into the online store. Anyway, when I was eleven I realised my dream was to make computers work like the human brain. I wanted computers to become more natural in the way they put ideas into practice. In today's world this is called 'deep learning'.

Man What is 'deep learning'?

Amrita Deep learning is a machine learning technique that teaches computers to do what comes naturally to humans: learn, for example. It is the key technology behind cars with no driver which can recognise road signs. It is what enables you to control devices like phones, TVs and air conditioning with your voice. Deep learning is getting lots of attention and for a good reason. It's achieving results that were not possible before, thanks to artificial intelligence.

Man What is life like for a teenager like you?

Amrita Well, although I'm the youngest person working for an international software company, I'm an average 15-year-old girl. I still enjoy hanging out with my friends, watching movies and playing with my sisters. And I'm still a student, though I don't go to school: I have four tutors teaching me subjects that I have to learn to take exams at the end of the school year. Of course, I don't need to learn much about maths and technology. In fact I have an online channel with over a hundred videos where I teach information technology.

Man So what are your plans for the future, Amrita?

Amrita Well, I really enjoy writing. I've already published a book where I explain artificial intelligence to teens like me and I'm going to write a second one, maybe about deep learning. I would also like to develop new computer games, but I don't think I'll have time to do that before the end of high school. Then I'll definitely go to university because I'd like to develop software that people can use to stay healthy.

Test 7

🔊 25 Part 1 p. 136

Rubric 1: What does Jane's grandfather look like now?

Callum Is this your father, Jane? He looks different with a beard.

Jane No Callum, that's my grandpa: he was handsome, wasn't he?

Callum Yes, I suppose so. When was this photo taken?

Jane Hmmm…. I think he was in his thirties in this picture so about 40 years ago. And that's my dad sitting in my grandma's arms.

Callum How old is he now?

Jane Older! He still looks great for his age, though he's shaved off his beard and… all his hair is gone.

Rubric 2: How much does the boy have to pay for his ticket?

Student Hello, how much are the tickets to the musical in Hall 1?

Assistant Well, it depends when you want to go.

Student Ah, OK. What's the difference in price?

Assistant Normally, the luxury seats cost £13.00 and standard seats are £8.00. But on Student's Fridays, all standard seats cost £5.00.

Student Well, I was going to come tomorrow, but as it's Friday I'll go this afternoon instead! Just a standard seat please for the 2 p.m. show.

Rubric 3: Which birthday present is Andrea wearing?

Thomas Hi, Andrea. How did you spend your birthday?

Andrea It was great. I had lunch at my aunt's in the countryside and had a big garden party with my classmates.

Thomas I guess you got loads of presents…

Andrea I did and they were all lovely. My aunt gave me this sweatshirt and my best friend's gift was a lovely set with a necklace and matching earrings: I can't wait to wear them later.

Thomas How about the hat you're wearing? Is that new too?

Andrea No, this is my brother's: I borrowed it today because I was a bit cold.

Rubric 4: How did the book end?

Girl Jerry, did you read the novel the literature teacher assigned last week?

Boy Yes, I did, but I was rather disappointed by the ending, though.

Girl Disappointed? Why? It's a very famous book, it won an award last year.

Boy Um, well, I didn't expect the man to be arrested and sent to jail: I mean, I was hoping he and the woman would fall in love and get married after they had spent two weeks travelling in the same car.

Girl Well, maybe this is not the end of the whole story.

Boy Why?

Girl You know, they say the author will probably write a second book next year, where there will be a spectacular plot twist.

Rubric 5: When is the wedding anniversary?

John What shall we do for mum and dad's wedding anniversary?

Richard I don't know. I was thinking we could organise a secret party on the 4th of March.

John But didn't they get married on the 1st?

Richard Yes, that's the date of their anniversary, but that's a weekday, so not many people would be able to come, and we've got a school exam on the Friday the 3rd. The 4th is a Saturday: that's the most convenient day for a party.

Rubric 6: What should the girl do first?

Teacher Ok, class, as I explained last week, we're preparing baked fish in salt today. It's quite easy. You clean the fish and put it in the oven to bake for 50 minutes.

Sue So what do we do with the salt, then, Sir?

Teacher We have to cover the fish in salt before baking it, of course. When you take it out of the oven, you throw away the salt crust and then add the tomatoes sauce.

Rubric 7: Which film have they just seen?

Robert How did you like the movie?

Lucy Mmm… I don't know…. I found some parts pretty boring: I mean, I really enjoyed the places, but the acting was poor: I almost fell asleep when Luke was in his tent in the woods.

Robert Yeah, Maybe they should have cut that part a little. They could have made him climb the old tower, at least. A bit more of action.

Lucy Oh, you're right, but I thought it would end with the love story between Luke and Anna.

Robert That was impossible: they couldn't stand each other!

🔊 26 Part 2 p. 138

Question 8

Linda James, what do you think of our new Drama teacher?

James Um, I think I like her. Don't you?

Linda Oh, yeah, I like how she dresses: she has very good taste.

James Actually, I was thinking about her teaching skills…

Transcripts

Linda Oh, she's fantastic: I totally love how she talks!
James Yeah, she's very good. But sometimes I can't understand some of the things she explains.
Linda Maybe you should pay more attention: she's very clear.

Question 9
Vic So, Aaron, how are you feeling after your camping holiday?
Aaron Oh Vic, I'm so tired! I've never slept in a tent before, I missed my bed so much!
Vic Really? I know it can be hard, at first, but it's not so bad.
Aaron It wasn't the best thing, definitely. But at least the weather was nice! And the people, too.
Vic Well, you were lucky: last time I went camping, my tent mates snored all the time. It was terrible!

Question 10
Martha Callum, please, switch to Channel4: 'Songs of the week' starts in a couple of minutes.
Callum Ugh, no, please: that programme is terrible. I'm not going to watch it.
Martha But Callum, it's my favourite programme!
Callum I know, but I can't stand it. Why don't we watch that new documentary about sea pollution? It's more interesting.
Martha Yes, it is. You're right. I can watch my music programme later this evening. But the documentary starts in 10 minutes: let's have a look at the news, first.
Callum What? The news? How boring!
Martha No, they are not! Here, listen: there's a train strike, tomorrow…

Question 11
Mum Good morning Tara. How was Jeannie's party yesterday?
Girl Well, it was nice.
Mum Were there many people?
Girl Um, yes. Maybe a bit too many, but it was fun. The music was terrific, and the food was good, too. But the cake wasn't sweet enough.
Mum Really?
Girl Yeah, I think the dark chocolate was too bitter!

Question 12
Dad Karen, are you ready to go on the school trip?
Karen Yeah, but I feel a bit sad.
Dad Sad? Why? Aren't you happy about it?
Karen Oh, yeah, I am. But I'm worried about Tobey. Will he miss me? Will he forget me?
Dad Oh, don't worry: your puppy won't forget you over the weekend! And he will be more than happy when you come back!
Karen Are you sure?
Dad Of course! Now, let's get into the bus: they are waiting for you!

Question 13
Greg Where shall we go for dinner? I want to try somewhere new.
Clara Actually, I don't fancy anything too strange.
Greg So, no sushi from the new Sushi Bar?
Clara Not really: Ann and Tony went just yesterday, and they felt ill just after it!
Greg Um, OK. But I don't feel like our usual hamburger and chips.
Clara You don't? OK. Why don't we go to the new pizzeria in Russell Square? I've heard they have special offers for new customers.
Greg Fine! Pizza it is!

 **Part 3 p. 139**
Man Good morning. Welcome to the International Film Museum. Our location in Marlene Dietrich Square, close to where the famous International Film Festival takes place every year, makes our museum a popular place to visit for tourists in Berlin. I'd like to give you some information to help you make this visit an unforgettable multimedia experience. Our permanent exhibition 'Film' on the first floor explains how movie making was born and developed as an art. In our 13 halls you will find over 1,000 exhibits from film scripts to costumes and props; you will learn about the development of filmmaking from the silent era to the special effects of the digital age. And don't miss the classic German film 'Metropolis' directed by Fritz Lang in 1927. On the second floor you will find a special section that is devoted to the greatest German actress of the big screen – Marlene Dietrich – with a number of her personal objects and memorabilia on show. On the same floor there is also a section on Science fiction and film animation. If you feel like a snack after the tour you can enjoy a hot cup of tea or some tasty German pastries at our bistro on the ground floor behind the ticket office. Before leaving don't forget to take a look in our museum shop next to the ticket office. For any information on the exhibits you can see in the museum check our online web page at www.germanfilmfest.de.

 **Part 4 p. 140**
Woman Today we're here with Luke Culotta who has become one of the most creative inventors in Europe. How did you first think about inventing things as a profession, Luke?
Luke Well, as a child I didn't use to be creative and I was quite lazy. The only thing I wanted when I left school was to set up my own business, so I started thinking about what I could do. My sister was making pretty slippers using women's old tights so I thought I could try selling them. She made a dozen pairs and I took them to a local street fair. When I got back home I was really happy. Though I had only sold three pairs, I had really enjoyed making things people found useful.
Woman So Luke, how did you manage to sell your first invention?
Luke The first thing I came up with was the 'Pelé football goal set'. I used a mini goal set that I played football with in my room. What I did was simply to stick a poster of my favourite footballer behind the goal net: I took a picture of my invention and sent it in to a toy company. It was an overnight success: my invention was on TV and magazine ads. In the first year I earned over 50 thousand pounds. So, you see, it wasn't really an invention: it was just a thing the market wanted and people bought it.
Woman What other things have you invented?
Luke One of the first products I invented was the 'Hug me cushion'. I was paid 25 thousand pounds for that idea, which was actually just a pair of arms on a pillow that you could hug while sleeping! I also made a talking watch for children, which was sold in toy stores for about 10 years. An invention that I was really proud of was the dog umbrella, but I found out that someone else had made it a few years before me. Though I didn't earn anything with it, it was definitely the more fun to create.
Woman I know inventing things is not the only thing you do. What else are you working on?
Luke Well, 15 years ago I set up a company: it was a school called 'Edison's Academy' where I trained people who wanted to invent things. Today I have several schools in Europe with hundreds of students aged from 14 to 80 years old.
Woman What is your most important suggestion to someone with an invention to sell?
Luke Most people think you should get a patent in order to stop anyone from stealing your idea. I agree on this point, though my number-one tip is to get in touch with companies and show them your idea, sending your project to the person in charge of new products development. Then you must obviously apply for a patent: since the rules change in the different countries, I suggest you check them online.
Woman What do you think the best and the worst inventions of the time are?
Luke The Internet. It is a shocking invention. I didn't see it coming and I didn't realise how amazing it would be; it's the largest library in the world and it allows me to do research, meet people and run a company that works in different countries. As for the worst one, it's the Internet again! No, actually, it's smartphones. They make everybody stressed out and in the end we have very little time to spend with real people. I think we need to get back to talking to each other more.

Transcripts

Test 8

 Part 1 p. 156

Rubric 1: Where is the washing machine?
Girl I do like your new flat! The kitchen's really big. But where are you going to put the washing machine?
Boy Didn't you see it? It's over there, between the fridge and the cooker, under the shelf with those plants on it.
Girl Oh! … I can't say I noticed!
Boy Well, my parents were right, then! It really goes unnoticed. Come on, I'll show you the rest of the house.

Rubric 2: Which team is she in?
Girl Well, I'm not playing tennis any more. It was getting really boring. And I've never liked jogging or athletics.
Boy So, what sport are you doing this year?
Girl Well, you know they asked me to play for the hockey team! Well, I said 'no' because although I am playing a bit of hockey, I'm in the football team now, and I can't play in both, can I?
Boy That's right. But you can always join them next year.

Rubric 3: Where are they going this weekend?
Mum I'm so tired! I think I need a break. Why don't we all go away this weekend?
Boy OK. Where do you want to go? To your sister's in Cambridge?
Mum That's not very original – we always go to your aunt's. And I don't want to be in a busy town full of tourists. What about that place on the coast? It's not far.
Boy Or we could go walking in the hills?
Mum I think relaxing by the sea is a better idea. I'm too exhausted to go walking!

Rubric 4: What did she buy?
Girl Hi! I'm back!
Boy Where have you been?
Girl Oh! You know I planned to go shopping with Mark!
Boy Oh yes! Did you get anything nice?
Girl Well, he bought a new hat, a scarf, and a couple of ties. He's got so much money to spend! I just got a pair of gloves: it's so cold these days. I wanted a dress, but everything's so expensive …

Rubric 5: How did they find out about the story?
Boy It's incredible, isn't it? What a story!
Girl Yes. I'm glad you switched the radio on. They never tell you these things on television. And you can't believe what they put in the newspapers.
Boy That's true. No story in the newspaper seems true to me.
Girl But you're always reading the paper!
Boy Well … only the sports pages!

Rubric 6: What should they move?
Woman OK. I want you to keep your arms out and your back straight. Now bend your head back and breathe slowly. It's important your back stays in position.
Boy This way?
Woman Well done! Oh, don't let those arms down! That's right.

Rubric 7: What is he going to do tomorrow?
Girl What are you doing tomorrow, Dad? It's a holiday!
Dad Well, I'm not going to clean the kitchen or the garage or anything like that! I want to relax a bit. I could have a game of golf, but I'll certainly spend some time in the garden.
Girl Oh, I thought you wanted to repair the car!
Dad But it's a holiday tomorrow! I'll repair it next week.
Girl Oh but Dad! I thought you were going to drive me to the cinema!

 **Part 2 p. 158**

Question 8
Boy Hi Mum! I'm home!
Mum Oh, hello, Andy. Tell me all about the school trip.
Boy Well, the journey was really long, but we played on our smartphones and chatted so it was OK.
Mum So what about the places you visited? Did you see lots of interesting things?
Boy Well… if you like museums, you'd have loved it. We went to the science museum first, which was great, then the natural history museum, then the technology museum…
Mum Oh that sounds lovely.
Boy Yeah, but we didn't do anything in the city at all apart from visit museums. The teachers just wanted us to do that all the time.

Question 9
Girl Hey, guess what! I've just joined the martial arts club at the gym!
Boy Good! I've heard it's great there. So what kind of things can you do?
Girl Well, I'm going to be very busy: I'm going to try karate on Tuesday, but I'm also going to do judo three times a week. And there are four kickboxing lessons every week if I can find the time…
Boy Wow! That's a lot!
Girl Yeah, it is. But I'm so happy I can't wait!
Boy Sounds like you'll be very tired, at the end of the week.

Question 10
Girl How are your violin lessons going, John?
Boy Hmmm, not that well. I want to get better, but I feel like I'm not making much progress.
Girl Well maybe you should practise more. It's a really difficult instrument and it takes a lot of effort to learn it well.
Boy I know, but I'm always practising! I just can't get enthusiastic about classical music.
Girl Well, I think you should look on the Internet and find videos of people playing different kinds of music. You could get some ideas of other styles to try.
Boy Yes, maybe you're right.

Question 11
Boy I've just finished reading this book. Have you read it? I thought it was a bit long, but it was a great story.
Girl Ah, yes, I read it last month. It didn't seem that long to me, it only took me two days to read it. I didn't think much of the ending, though.
Boy Why not? I liked it. I didn't expect the girl to come back at all so it was a big surprise!
Girl Well, I guessed that would happen from the start. I liked the characters though. A lot of them reminded me of people that I know.
Boy Yeah, me too ... In fact I thought the girl was a lot like you!
Girl Really? I'm not sure if that's a compliment or not!

Question 12
Girl Well! That's definitely the last time I'm paying to see that band! What a load of rubbish! It wasn't worth half of what we paid.
Boy Yeah, it was definitely too expensive, but I didn't think they played badly. The guitarist was really great, and the others played well too.
Girl Well, I think I could have played better than them! And the instruments were far too loud. I couldn't even hear the singer most of the time!
Boy Hmm, that's true. It wasn't great sound quality, was it?
Girl Maybe we should ask for our money back!

Question 13
Boy Hey Amy, look at my new smartphone.
Girl Wow, it looks great. I love the colour, and it's much bigger than mine.
Boy Yeah I asked for this size because it's more practical for surfing the Internet. But the main reason why I chose this one is because the sound quality is so good for when I listen to my favourite bands.
Girl And what about the camera? Does it take good photos?
Boy Actually, I'm not so sure about that. I don't think the quality's quite as good as on my last phone, but I don't usually take many photos anyway so that doesn't really matter.
Girl Really? That would be the most important thing for me.

Part 3 p. 159
Man Hi everyone! Now listen carefully, because it's time for me to give you the details of our latest competition. It's for all you young artists out there! This is The Fifth Annual Sound Radio Drawing and Painting Competition! Get a pencil, and write

175

down the information you need to enter. First things first: the competition is only open to young people up to the age of 21, so all you oldies will have to find somewhere else to send your works of art! There is a special category for those under 10 years old, so do make sure you fill in the box indicating your age. That reminds me! To enter, you must, I repeat, must send an application form, completed and with an adult's signature, if you're under 16. If you're over 16 you can sign it yourself. What should you send us? Well, there are three categories in each age group: pencil drawings, watercolours and 'experimental'. Don't ask me what the last one means: it's up to you! You can use anything you like to make a picture. We've had some strange materials used by competitors in the past, I can tell you! Now the most important information of all: the winner will be announced on the 15th July, but the final date for you to send your work is the 30th of June, so you need to get started as soon as possible. Remember, you can send as many pictures as you like. We are happy to see all the art we can get from our listeners. Oh yes! The prizes: luxury radios for the top ten in each category, painting sets for the works considered of above average quality by the judges, and for the number one winner, the chance to see his or her work put up on the wall in our entrance hall. It will be there for ever, for any visitor to admire.

Part 4 p. 160

Interviewer Good afternoon, Mr Bell. Here is our first question: what are climate change and global warming, and how are they related?

Mr Bell Global warming refers to an increase in average global temperatures, which in turn causes climate change. Climate change refers to changes in seasonal temperature, precipitation, wind, and humidity for a given area. Climate change can involve cooling or warming. Temperature studies show that average global temperatures have risen since the industrial revolution began, with increases accelerating over the past few decades and most of the increase is due to human economic activity, especially to burning of fossil fuels and deforestation. These activities contribute to a build-up in carbon dioxide (CO_2) and other gases in Earth's atmosphere.

Interviewer Which countries contribute the most to global warming?

Mr Bell Wealthier industrial countries contribute the most to global warming since they use most of the world's fossil fuels. Europe, Japan, and North America—with roughly 15% of the world's current population—are estimated to account for two-thirds of the carbon dioxide now in the atmosphere. With less than 5% of world population, the United States is the single-largest source of carbon from fossil fuels—emitting 24% of the world's total. U.S. vehicles emit roughly as much carbon as the entire Japanese economy, the world's fourth-largest carbon emitter in 2000. China, despite being home to one-fifth of the world's population and its heavy dependence on coal, ranks a distant second behind the U.S., emitting 12% of the global total. The average person in China produces less than one-eighth as much carbon dioxide as the average American.

Interviewer What can we do right now to slow climate change and make a real difference?

Mr Bell While it's impossible for any one individual to prevent global warming, we each have a direct impact on the conditions that allow warming to occur. We can do our part to conserve energy and pollute less. Whether at home, on our commute to work or school, in the office, or at the store, there are things we can do to lessen our contribution to climate change.

Ready for B1 Preliminary *for Schools*

Editorial coordination: Simona Franzoni
Editorial department: Simona Bagalà, Sara Bennett
Art Director: Marco Mercatali
Page layout: Federico Borsella
Picture Editor: Giorgia D'Angelo
Illustrations: Massimo Carriero
Production Manager: Francesco Capitano
Cover design: Curvilinee

© 2019 ELI S.r.l
P.O. Box 6
62019 Recanati
Italy
Tel. +39 071 750701
Fax. +39 071 977851
info@elionline.com
www.elionline.com

Third reprint June 2024

Acknowledgements
Photos: Shutterstock

No unauthorised photocopying.
All rights reserved. No part of this publication may be reproduced, stored in a retrieval system, or transmitted, in any form or by any means, electronic, mechanical, photocopying, recording or otherwise, without the prior written permission of ELI.
This book is sold subject to the condition that it shall not, by way of trade or otherwise, be lent, resold, hired out, or otherwise circulated without the publisher's prior consent in any form of binding or cover than that in which it is published and without a similar condition being imposed on the subsequent purchaser.

While every effort has been made to trace all the copyright holders, if any have been inadvertently overlooked the publisher will be pleased to make the necessary arrangements at the first opportunity.

Printed in Italy by Tecnostampa – Pigini Group Printing Division
Loreto – Trevi 19.83.474.2

ISBN: 978-88-536-2787-2